THE ART OF BALANCE

STAYING SANE IN AN INSANE WORLD

DAVID J. BOOKBINDER

ILLUSTRATIONS BY STEPHANIE BOND

TRANSFORMATIONS PRESS

The information provided in this book is designed to provide helpful information on the subjects discussed. This book is not meant to be used, nor should it be used, to diagnose or treat any psychological or medical condition. The publisher and author are not liable for any damages or negative consequences from any treatment, action, application or preparation, to any person reading or following the information in this book. References are provided for informational purposes only and do not constitute endorsement of any websites or other sources. Readers should be aware that the websites listed in this book may change.

Published in Danvers, Massachusetts by Transformations Press.

Mail: Transformations Press
          85 Constitution Lane 300-C4
          Danvers, MA 01923
Phone: 978-395-1292
Email: info@transformationspress.org

Group: facebook.com/groups/balancelab
Blog: phototransformations.com
Books: transformationspress.org
Main: davidbookbinder.com

Library of Congress Control Number: 2017915908

Publisher's Cataloging-In-Publication Data

Names: Bookbinder, David J. | Bond, Stephanie, 1990- illustrator.
Title: The art of balance : staying sane in an insane world / David J. Bookbinder ; illustrations by Stephanie Bond.
Description: Danvers, Massachusetts : Transformations Press, [2018] | Includes bibliographical references.
Identifiers: ISBN 9780984699469 | ISBN 9780984699476 (ebook)
Subjects: LCSH: Peace of mind. | Well-being. | Stress management. | Resilience (Personality trait) | Mindfulness (Psychology) | Self-help techniques.
Classification: LCC BF637.P3 B66 2018 (print) | LCC BF637.P3 (ebook) | DDC 158.1--dc23

Printed in the United States of America.

Other Books by David J. Bookbinder

Nonfiction Books

Paths to Wholeness: Fifty-Two Flower Mandalas

What Folk Music is All About

The Lotus Guide to 1-2-3

Coloring Books

52 Flower Mandalas: An Adult Coloring Book for Inspiration and Stress Relief

52 (more) Flower Mandalas: An Adult Coloring Book for Inspiration and Stress Relief

Other Transformations Press Books

Fiction by Eugene K. Garber

Metaphysical Tales

The Historian

Beasts in Their Wisdom

Vienna ØØ

O Amazonas Escuro

The House of Nordquist

The greatest victory is that which requires no battle.

- **Sun Tzu,** *The Art of War*

CONTENTS

Author's Note   vi
Introduction   ix
The Cast of Characters   1
    Al and Alice   2
    UnBalancer   3
    Balancer   4
    ReBalancer   5
    Balanced, UnBalanced, ReBalanced   6
Part I. Balance Lost   7
    1. Things Fall Apart   8
Part II. Balance Regained   13
    2. The Balancer/ReBalancer Tag Team   14
    3. ReBalancer to the Rescue   17
    4. Assess and Plan   25
    5. Restore Balance   37
    6. The Experiment   46
Part III. Balance Maintained   57
    7. The Balancer/ReBalancer Loop   58
    8. Build Resilience   68
    9. Manage and Reduce Stress   73
    10. Rebalance Your Brain   78
    11. Build Connections and Support   85
    12. Embrace Change   89
    13. Mix in Mindfulness   107
    14. Uncertainty, Allies, and Confederates   114
    15. Stay Sane with the Personal Craziness Index   122
Wrap-Up: Balance Lost, Regained, Maintained   131
Addendum: When UnBalancer is the Hero   150
Acknowledgments   154
Thank You!   156
About the Author   157

Author's Note

Balance is a word with many meanings, in many contexts. But in May, 1971, when I was a college sophomore, it meant "to become more complete."

That's when I started on a four-month hitch-hiking journey across the United States, following a meandering loop west from Buffalo to Berkeley, south past L.A., up the coasts of California, Oregon, and Washington, and back east through Canada.

I started that trip wanting to see the country, but I quickly understood I was really on a mission to balance out who I was.

My travels included many adventures I still vividly recall, but more importantly, they gave me an expanded outlook I have carried with me all my life.

I began that trip with $400 and a sense of adventure. I returned with 25 cents in my pocket and a new vision of who I could become. It's the best $399.75 investment I've ever made.

Within days of my return, I made a list of new activities to undertake. On it were writing, photography, learning a trade, practicing a sport, pursuing a spiritual activity, and, to carry on the traveler's sense of adventure, motorcycling. This list became the curriculum for a program to rebalance myself that, in a more nuanced way, I'm still following today.

That semester, I started to carry out my curriculum, setting aside physics and calculus courses and exchanging them for the humanities, and seeking out new-to-me activities that would, I hoped, enhance my undeveloped physical, emotional, spiritual, and creative sides.

I took all the literature, philosophy, psychology, and creative writing courses I could fit into my schedule. I volunteered at a mental hospital and at a faculty-run free school. I started to make knives as a hobby. I played tennis, rode a motorcycle, practiced Transcendental Meditation. I apprenticed in carpentry and used that skill to put myself through school and, for several years after graduation, to support my new writing and photography habits.

Books have long been the first step into activities that have extended me. They were part of my curriculum then, and they are still part of it now.

Before I looked for a job as a carpenter's apprentice, I read books on woodworking. Before I volunteered at a state mental hospital, I read from the founders of Western psychology. Before I made my first knife, I read a book on metallurgy. Before I taught my first class, I studied up on pedagogy. After a near-death experience altered the way I think and feel, books were where I went to help understand what had happened to me, and it was a book by Carl Rogers that convinced me to become a therapist.

I have almost no sense of direction, but I'm very good at reading maps, and books are, for me, the most elaborate and detailed maps to just about everything. In my travels through time since my trip across the United States, they have guided me to places I would never have ventured without their gentle prodding.

In *The Art of Balance: Staying Sane in an Insane World*, I've distilled the best of what I've learned from my own experiences as a person and a therapist, and from the best teachers I know. I hope this book—and the cast of characters it contains—will help to guide you on the hills and valleys of your own unique journey.

- David J. Bookbinder

Introduction

He who only sees the obvious, wins his battles with difficulty. He who looks below the surface of things, wins with ease.

- **Sun Tzu**, *The Art of War*

Sometimes the stresses of life wear us down. Sometimes, they knock us off our feet. Either way, we can lose our balance, and if we fall hard enough, it can take a long time to get back up.

The Battle for Balance is a life and death struggle: Stay balanced, and we enjoy life to the fullest. Lose balance, and things get hard.

In this book, I'm going to show you how to stay on top of the forces that unbalance us, how to recover if you do get knocked down, and how to build resilience so you're better prepared the next time the forces of imbalance—let's call them *unbalancers*—throw you a curve ball.

I help people rebalance their lives every day.

As a life coach and therapist, I've had more than 15 years of real-world experience helping people successfully overcome a wider range of unbalancers than most people encounter in a lifetime.

Together, we deal with problems large and small, immediate and chronic. Using the methods in this book, my clients not only recover from whatever brought them down, they also grow more insightful, more resilient to stress, and better able to make choices that bring them happiness and well-being.

The Art of Balance: Staying Sane in an Insane World is different from self-help articles and books you may have seen before. And, if I can blow my own horn for a moment, it's better.

Unlike most articles on the Internet and a lot of self-help books, *The Art of Balance* provides much more than a laundry list of the "Top 10 (or 25, or 100) Tools and Techniques."

It's not a greatest hits. It's a system.

It's a system that will help you recognize the forces that knock us out of balance, outline a strategy for overcoming them, and adopt a methodology for achieving lasting balance. The self-help tools and techniques are in there, sure, but they are integrated into a framework that also teaches you how to create your own tools, develop your own techniques, and refine your own strategies—and thereby become the master of your destiny.

The Art of Balance doesn't "give a man a fish," so he can eat that day. It teaches you how to fish. It's a system you can adapt not only to the issues you face today, but also to the unknown unknowns you may face as you move through your life.

These time-tested strategies have helped hundreds of my clients—and they've also helped me. To paraphrase the old "hair club for men" ads on late-night television, "I'm not only the therapist, I'm also a client."

Many of the lessons in *The Art of Balance* I learned through my own struggles with unbalancers. I've been knocked flat by relationships and health crises, worn down by burnout and wrong career choices, and deeply shaken by accidents, crime, losing people close to me, and my own close brush with death. Not to mention more than my fair share of mistakes, large and small.

All of these experiences have been teachers, and the lessons learned from them have given me insights, heightened my intuition, and taught me skills that have benefited my clients—and will soon help you.

I often tell my clients, "I can save you 10 or 20 years of trial and error." *The Art of Balance* can save *you* 10 or 20 years, too.

They say that "what does not kill you makes you stronger," but this saying is only true if you know how to turn adversity into opportunity, and you learn from your difficult experiences.

The balance strategies and tools you're about to discover will teach you how to do that. No book can provide all the answers, but the methods you learn here will give you the confidence to handle, adroitly, whatever situations come your way.

The word "overwhelmed" will no longer be in your vocabulary.

Instead, when you follow the steps revealed in *The Art of Balance*, you're sure to move forward with a spring in your step that won't get unsprung.

The Cast of Characters

Know thy self, know thy enemy.
- **Sun Tzu**, *The Art of War*

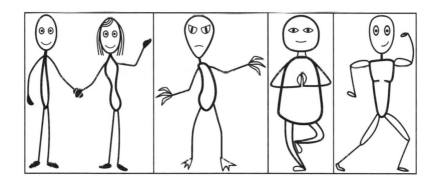

This is a book about balance: what disrupts it, what restores it, and how to keep it going.

It is also a story.

And like any story, it has its cast of characters. Some are friends and fellow travelers. Some are enemies. In the pages of this book, you will come to know them well.

But first, some introductions.

AL AND ALICE

We are the heroes of this saga, an epic battle not only for balance but literally for life, liberty, and the pursuit of happiness.

UNBALANCER

The villain in our story is the nefarious **UnBalancer**.

UnBalancer is a fearsome and sometimes deadly force. It strives single-mindedly to unseat us, and sometimes it wins the battle— but not, as we'll see, the war.

BALANCER

Our chief ally in combating UnBalancer is **Balancer.**

Balancer is the internal stabilizer that handles day-to-day stresses. It keeps us sane and balanced most of the time and, for the most part, holds UnBalancer at bay.

Emphasis on "for the most part." When Balancer falls, things can get wonky fast.

ReBalancer

Fortunately, Balancer is not our only ally.

Balancer's trusty sidekick, **ReBalancer**, leaps into action when UnBalancer gets the upper hand.

ReBalancer is a good friend to have in a crisis.

Balanced, UnBalanced, ReBalanced

Here's how these folks work to keep us sane.

1. Balancer operates in the background to maintain our equilibrium.

2. UnBalancer trips us up!

3. ReBalancer comes to the rescue.

4. A stronger, wiser Balancer keeps us stable again.

PART I.
BALANCE LOST

If you know the enemy and know yourself, you need not fear the result of a hundred battles.

If you know yourself but not the enemy, for every victory gained you will also suffer a defeat.

If you know neither the enemy nor yourself, you will succumb in every battle.

- **Sun Tzu**, *The Art of War*

1. THINGS FALL APART

Disorder came from order, fear came from courage, weakness came from strength.

- **Sun Tzu**, *The Art of War*

"The Under Toad," Walt said. "I'm trying to see it. How big is it?"

And Garp and Helen and Duncan held their breath; they realized that all these years Walt had been dreading a giant toad, lurking offshore, waiting to suck him under and drag him out to sea. The terrible Under Toad.

Garp tried to imagine it with him. Would it ever surface? Did it ever float? Or was it always down under, slimy and bloated and ever-watchful for ankles its coated tongue could snare? The vile Under Toad.

In John Irving's novel *The World According to Garp*, the Under Toad is a monster young Walt Garp imagined when he misunderstood a warning to beware of the undertow. For Walt's parents, T. S. and Helen Garp, it becomes a code word for anxiety. *"When the traffic was heavy, when the road was icy—when depression had moved in overnight—they said to each other, 'The Under Toad is strong today.'"*

Enter: UnBalancer

In the physical world, things go out of balance when there's a design flaw, when something breaks, when unequal forces press on an object. Imbalance typically worsens over time, gradually compromising the whole structure.

An unbalanced tire rattles the car. A leak in a roof leads to a ceiling falling in. When winds vibrated the Tacoma Narrows bridge to its resonant frequency in 1940, the whole structure danced briefly and then catastrophically collapsed. When an O-ring failed in the Space Shuttle Challenger, the spacecraft exploded.

The same thing happens to us, individually and collectively, when the forces that throw us out of balance are at play. We begin to wear and to ripple, sometimes to the point of collapse, sometimes to explosion.

These myriad forces have a common root in **UnBalancer**.

UnBalancer is *not only* Chaos, though Chaos can be its confederate, nor is it *only* Accident, Misfortune, Entropy, Chance, Obliviousness, Fear, Greed, Distrust, Anger, Hatred, Passion, Illness, or any of the other internal and external forces that sometimes knock us out of alignment.

It's all of these things, and it's also more.

Sometimes UnBalancer is blunt and direct. When life takes a turn for the worse—we lose a job, a relationship, or suddenly face a difficult health problem—UnBalancer rubs its hands in glee. When sudden tragedy strikes, UnBalancer does handstands and turns cartwheels, jumping for joy.

But more often, the forces of UnBalancer are subtle. Even when nothing is obviously going wrong, UnBalancer is a magician who draws our attention to whatever's in the foreground so it can work its mischief unseen.

UnBalancer is patient.

Like the frog (or toad) contentedly sitting in a pot of gradually heating water, unaware it's about to get cooked, the path to imbalance is often almost imperceptible at first. When the books are out of balance, for example, the road to ruin may already be paved, but nobody notices. The sh*t hits the fan when there's nothing left to borrow. Witness the financial collapse of 1929. Or 2008.

On a global scale, the inventions of agriculture and manufacturing have, over thousands of years, altered the environment, unbalancing the Earth itself.

In our individual lives, when the teeter-totter of work and leisure gets too heavily weighted toward one or the other, things go awry. When our diet gets out of sync with the nutrients our bodies need to function, our health starts to break down. The same goes for imbalance in waking and sleeping, thinking and doing, yin and yang.

UnBalancer revels in our unawareness.

UnBalancer is strong today.

So how do we reckon with it?

Stay tuned!

PART II.
BALANCE REGAINED

Anger may in time change to gladness; vexation may be succeeded by contentment.

- **Sun Tzu**, *The Art of War*

2. THE BALANCER/REBALANCER TAG TEAM

The Art of War teaches us to rely not on the likelihood of the enemy's not coming, but on our own readiness to receive him; not on the chance of his not attacking, but rather on the fact that we have made our position unassailable.

- **Sun Tzu**, *The Art of War*

As powerful as UnBalancer is, and as insidious, each of us has powerful allies to help us counteract it. One of them is **Balancer**.

Balancer Defined

Like UnBalancer, Balancer is a multifaceted entity.

Balancer is not *only* Awareness, though Awareness is certainly one of its components. It's not just Mindfulness, either, though Mindfulness can be a powerful aid in maintaining balance. Nor is it fully defined by Logic, Intuition, Common Sense, Moderation, Resilience, or any of the other functions that help us maintain equilibrium.

It's all of these, and more.

Balancer functions much like the immune system, which automatically monitors our internal and external environments and correctly sorts out, *most of the time*, what's us and what's not, what's good for us and what isn't. Or like the pancreas, which in a healthy body automatically regulates, *most of the time*, the balance of sugar and insulin that is essential for survival.

Balancer Overcome

For most of us, Balancer does a good job handling routine stresses. It efficiently deals with assaults on balance such as minor illnesses, disappointments, bad weather, an argument, a too-short night or a too-long day. When these events occur, Balancer automatically compensates, much as a gyroscope can right itself when it's nudged one way or another. But if the stress is too much or goes on for too long, Balancer can be overpowered.

And then we start to tilt.

That's when Balancer's more adroit partner, **ReBalancer**, fires its retro rockets.

ReBalancer is the composite of the tools, techniques, strategies, actions, and supports we've acquired so that we can restabilize when UnBalancer pushes us too hard, too suddenly, or for too long.

3. ReBalancer to the Rescue

Plan for what is difficult while it is easy, do what is great while it is small.

- **Sun Tzu**, *The Art of War*

When UnBalancer gets the better of us, ReBalancer's at our side, ready to help get us back on our feet.

Unlike Balancer, ReBalancer doesn't engage automatically. ReBalancer kicks in when we consciously initiate actions to get ourselves back into balance.

ReBalancer can save the day when Balancer fails to maintain our equilibrium. But, ReBalancer can come to the rescue *if*, and *only if*, three factors are in place:

1. **We realize we need ReBalancer's help.**

2. **ReBalancer is ready for action.**

3. **ReBalancer has, or can acquire, the skills to handle the situation.**

The stakes are high for maintaining balance. In my own life, UnBalancer has gotten the better of Balancer many, many times. Sometimes ReBalancer came to my aid, but when I was too slow in calling on it, or ReBalancer wasn't up to the task, things went south.

Here are a couple of examples of the Battle for Balance.

Diabetes

On a physical level, **Type II diabetes** is typical of a Balancer/UnBalancer duel where UnBalancer often gets the upper hand.

Approximately 10 million Americans have Type II diabetes, and another 90 million have prediabetes, a condition which typically morphs into diabetes within five years.

By the time people begin to show the early warning signs of prediabetes—high cholesterol and triglycerides, high blood pressure, episodes of low blood sugar, and a bit of fat around the middle—their bodies are already out of balance.

Calling on ReBalancer to take corrective actions with lifestyle changes such as modifying your diet, losing weight, and adding exercise can prevent onset of the disease. But many prediabetics and their doctors don't take these symptoms seriously enough until diabetes has set in and they are past the point of no return. Score one for UnBalancer!

Burnout

In our world of too much work and not enough play, another common example of UnBalancer on the move is **burnout.**

Burnout leads to depression, anxiety, and physical and emotional exhaustion. It hampers work, home life, and health, and it can undermine most of what we find satisfying in our lives.

As a psychotherapist in private practice, I understand all this. But knowledge alone doesn't convey immunity. Knowledge is helpful, but actions speak louder than words, as UnBalancer well knows.

In my therapy practice, I try to maintain a consistent number of clients. When people leave therapy, I take on new clients until my case load is where I want it, then I stop until I have more openings. My internal Balancer monitors my schedule and makes sure I don't see too few clients or add too many.

Sometimes, though, a major world or local event shakes people up and brings an unusual number of former clients back into therapy. Balancer can usually accommodate a few extra clients, but if I continue to add more, the work/downtime balance tips too far in the work direction.

I love my work; it has felt like a calling, and one I gladly answered. But too much of a good thing is still … too much.

A brutal winter that broke Boston's all-time seasonal snowfall record took its toll not only on the local economy, but also the local psyche. Every week for 14 weeks, former clients, some of whom I hadn't seen in years, called, emailed, and texted, asking to resume therapy. And because I had a policy of never turning away a former client, I accepted them. *All* of them.

Balancer's scheduling arm tried to compensate. It stuffed clients into gaps in my day normally devoted to paperwork and pushed the paperwork off to the weekend. When that wasn't enough to stem the tide of returning clients, Balancer added appointment hours to the end and then to the beginning of first one workday, then two, and eventually to all five.

While the scheduling arm handled those arrangements, another Balancer arm readjusted the rest of my life to compensate.

First, it made more efficient use of non-work time. Then, as the clients kept coming, it cut out downtime entirely, eliminating recreational activities, time with friends, and basic activities such as meal preparation, house cleaning, and car maintenance. When that still wasn't enough, it cut back on sleep.

You can see where this is going, but I didn't. Balancer was busy doing its valiant best to keep me keeping on, but my work schedule was grinding me to the bone.

Weeks turned into months, and clients I thought had returned for a brief tune-up stayed for a new therapy run, while the stream of returning clients continued. By the time the buds were on the trees I drove past on the way to my office, I was too tired and too wired on caffeine to notice.

UnBalancer was in charge and, to paraphrase the Irish poet William Butler Yeats, things fell apart, the center did not hold.

The first signs of burnout were subtle. I occasionally forgot an appointment or scheduled two people for the same time slot. I procrastinated on billing and sometimes missed the payment window with insurance companies. I put aside continuing education trainings until the last few months of the year, then had to cram them all in at once, further adding to my stress.

I slept poorly, drank more coffee to stay alert, and started needing brief naps between sessions. Each day was an uphill battle to stay awake, alert, and helpful to my too-many clients.

Though I didn't know it until my annual physical, my blood pressure had risen to dangerous levels. Only when a capillary in my retina leaked, causing a permanent blind spot, did Balancer pause from its frantic efforts and cry out, "Help!"

ReBalancer tried to come to the rescue, but it was sluggish, out of practice, and short on the skills needed to right the ship again.

UnBalancer won that round.

But not the war.

Eventually, clients completed their therapy and moved on. And slowly I, too, returned to homeostasis. A little beaten up, but a lot wiser.

What to Do When Things Fall Apart

When things fall apart, here's what ReBalancer must do if we're to pull ourselves together again:

1. **Detect.** Whether it's because Balancer notices that we're starting to tip or we've already gone down for the count, stop the action. You are now in crisis mode. Don't wander aimlessly, hoping to find a direction. Take a time out, even if the only place you can take it is in your mind.

2. **Assess.** You've been knocked off your feet and you need to know where you are before you can return to the ring. ReBalancer starts by assessing the damage and evaluating the options. Consider what went wrong that got you into this jam, then inventory the resources and supports you need to get back on your feet.

3. **Plan.** ReBalancer helps you strategize your recovery and get ready to take your first steps back.

4. **Restore.** ReBalancer patches up your cuts, ices your bruises, wraps your injured hands, makes sure you're steady on your feet and can see straight. Then it figures out how best to get back into the ring. The best place to start is with what you already know. If taking morning walks helped you start your day in the right frame of mind, start walking again. If getting a good night's sleep helped you deal better with a difficult time, address your sleep habits. If working out at the gym gave you energy and lifted your mood, go back to the gym.

You knew how to do what helped you before, and you'll know how to do it again.

If doing what you used to do isn't getting you where you want to go, **experiment**. Look at what helps others in similar situations. Add new activities and supports, one at a time, paying attention to what works for you and what doesn't. Apply course corrections as needed. The most basic rule of thumb to follow is: If it's working, do more of it or more things like it. If it's not, do something else. (See Chapter 6, "The Experiment.")

Still stuck? **Ask for help**. You don't have to do this all on your own. Ask friends, family, mentors. Check out support groups. Find an expert. As the great English poet John Donne put it, "No man is an island." Sometimes crisis makes us isolate, but isolation is not what we need to get through a crisis.

Burnout and ReBalancer

To illustrate, here's what eventually got me out of burnout, as my sluggish ReBalancer finally kicked into gear:

1. **Detect**. By late spring, I'd been unbalanced so long it looked like balanced to me. I took a few days off from my over-crowded schedule and rode my motorcycle out to the rural part of New York State where my brother and sister-in-law live. In this relaxing, no-pressure environment, I slept late, did a little writing, and glided through the rolling hills and low-key-lovely farms and towns. Each day there, I felt a little more human, and eventually I was able to recognize what had happened to me, and to embrace the burnout that was mine.

2. **Assess**. On the long, peaceful return trip through the Berk-shires and on to the Boston area, I started to see that I needed to add back the self-care strategies I'd left behind the previous winter, and that to do so I'd have to scale back my schedule. (See Chapter 5, "Restore Balance," for more on mini self-care.)

3. **Plan**. Using a shortened version of the Miracle Question, I envisioned a more balanced and healthier life and mapped out some of the first steps toward getting to it. (See Chapter 4, "Assess and Plan," for more on the Miracle Question.)

4. **Restore**. First, I stopped taking new clients, no matter how good a match I thought I was to their problems. Then I learned to say "Sorry, I can't see you right now, but I can book something two months from now" to clients who wanted to

return to therapy. I also cut my individual therapy sessions, which had crept up to an hour each, back to the 50 minutes that are the standard in my field.

As small spaces opened up in my schedule, I began to incorporate some of the restorative activities and practices I'd deleted from my life. These included brief versions of self-care activities, such as reading, taking photographs, meditating, meeting friends for meals, and taking short walks and motorcycle rides. And I reduced my caffeine intake and made sure I got at least seven hours sleep every night.

To free up more time, I **experimented** with something I'd never done before: I asked some clients who were not in a critical state if, instead of seeing me weekly, they wanted to go to biweekly, leaving open the option of coming weekly again if they really needed it. Several tried that, with good results.

To better prepare myself against future burnout, I also **asked for help**. I talked with my peer supervision group about their self-care and practice management strategies and took online trainings on burnout prevention.

Over the next few months, my sanity returned.

ReBalancer's Toolkit

In my profession, I typically see people when UnBalancer has had its way for a long time.

Fortunately, as a result of both my personal and professional battles, I've built up a toolkit to jumpstart recovery from the mischief—and sometimes the carnage—that UnBalancer creates.

In the next several chapters, I'll go into some of the most effective ReBalancer tools I've found to help work back to balance when UnBalancer has had its way.

4. Assess and Plan

Water shapes its course according to the nature of the ground over which it flows; the soldier works out his victory in relation to the foe whom he is facing.

- **Sun Tzu**, *The Art of War*

Before starting on any journey, most of us do some kind of planning. Where do we want to go? What route should we take? Who will be coming with us? What do we need to pack? What would we like to do when we get there?

Whether we've become unbalanced by the slow, erosive process of accumulated stress or by a sudden difficult event, at some point we need to ask ourselves a similar set of questions.

Each of the assessment tools in this chapter can help in the early stages of recovery from imbalance.

I've included a variety of methods here because the needs of each person are different at different times. If you're unsure which to try, try them all. None takes much time or effort, and each is effective in its own way.

The Medicine Wheel

The Medicine Wheel is a tool used by many Native American tribes.

Its basic form is a circle divided into four equal quadrants. Different tribes have ascribed different meanings to each of these quadrants, such as stages of life, seasons of the year, and elements of nature.

When you are recovering from UnBalancer's actions, you can use the medicine wheel to find the answers to what your mind/heart needs, what your body needs, what your spirit needs, and who can be an ally.

Begin by drawing a circle on a blank sheet of paper, then divide the circle into four quadrants. Write the words "Mind/Heart," "Body," "Spirit," and "Ally" in the four quadrants, as shown below.

With your eyes closed, ask yourself each of the following questions. Try not to answer with your thoughts. Instead, wait for images to come to mind. When an image forms, draw it in the appropriate quadrant, then write any words that came with them.

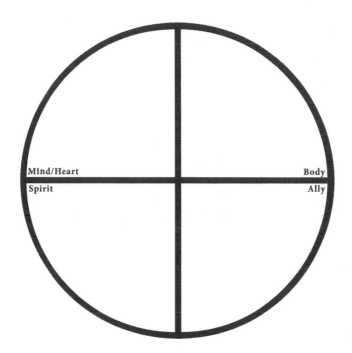

1. **What does your mind and heart need?** Draw what comes to you in the upper-left quadrant, then write the words that come with them.

2. **What does your body need?** In the upper-right quadrant, draw the answer to this question, then write your answer down in words.

3. **What does your spirit need?** In the lower-left quadrant, draw what comes to your imagination, and then write the words that accompany them.

4. **Who or what is your ally?** In the lower-right quadrant, draw the figure that appears in your mind, then write any words that come to you to describe it.

Here's a completed version of the Medicine Wheel I did as part of recovering from burnout. (For readability, I've replaced the handwritten words with type.):

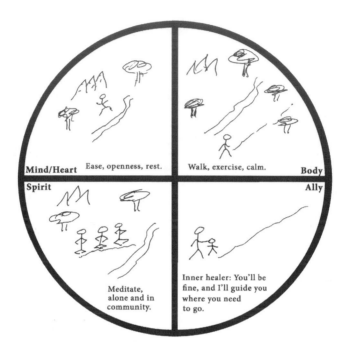

After you complete the exercise, give yourself time to let what you have discovered sink into your mind, heart, body, and spirit.

Circles of Problems and Resources

Even when we're down for the count, most of us have more capacity to deal with the things that unbalance us than we realize.

The Circles of Problems and Resources is a tool for inventorying our internal and external resources and envisioning how to use them to solve our problems.

Like the characters in the film *The Wizard of Oz*, whose Cowardly Lion receives a medal to show his courage, whose Tin Woodman gets a ticking clock to remind him of his compassionate nature, and whose Scarecrow is awarded a certificate to prove his intelligence, we, too, sometimes need a way to draw our attention to the resources we already have.

That's what completing the Circles of Problems and Resources does. It's a simple but powerful tool for quickly identifying the issues you're experiencing and the resources that can help you resolve them. It's perfect for taking inventory when you've been abandoned in the woods by UnBalancer.

To create it, begin by drawing a doughnut shape that fills most of the middle of a single sheet of paper.

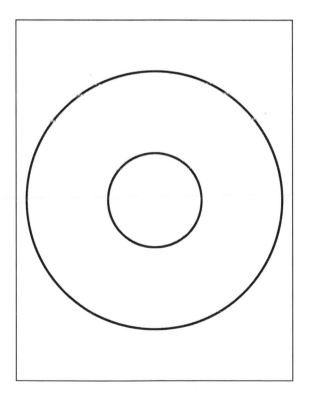

Inside the innermost circle, list the problems you are currently experiencing.

In the outer circle, list the internal resources that might help with these problems, and in the area outside the doughnut, list the external resources that also could be helpful.

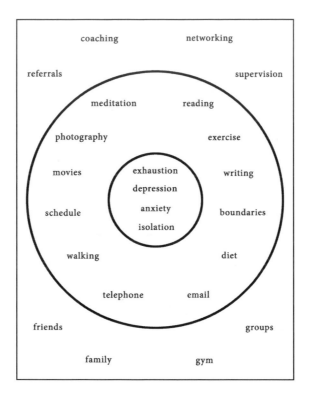

Finally, draw lines to connect each of the problems with your internal and external resources. These are the actions, activities, practices, and supports that can lead you out of UnBalancer's maze.

For instance, in the burnout example mentioned earlier, my primary symptoms were exhaustion, depression, and anxiety.

Here, I've linked exhaustion to the resources that helped with that aspect of the problem.

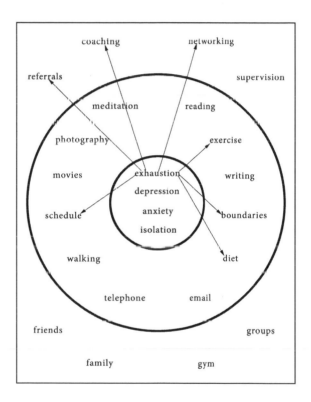

Once you've completed the Circles of Problems and Resources, you can use it as a map to guide you back to balance.

Turn the page for a completed version of the burnout example.

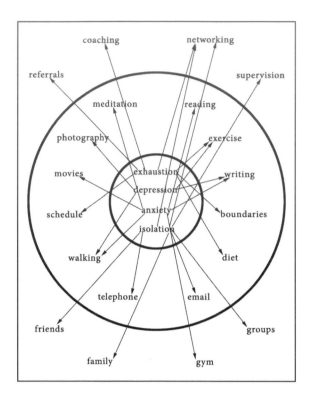

The Miracle Question

The tool I use most often to help my clients assess their problems and then forge a path to a better life is called the Miracle Question. It's one of the most effective questions I've encountered as a therapist. I wish I'd created it! (It was developed in the 1970s by Insoo Kim Berg and Steven de Shazer.)

Answering the Miracle Question is the first step on a path that can not only lead you back to equilibrium but, if you continue to work it, can take you to levels of life satisfaction you may never have experienced. It's a way to concretely envision what life will be like when your problems are solved and your current concerns are no longer concerning.

The Miracle Question is like the Call to Adventure that launches the Hero's Journey, a story structure that appears in myths and folktales from around the world. It impels us to take risks and endure struggles we might not otherwise have taken and endured, but which yield rewards that cannot be obtained any other way.

The Miracle Question goes like this:

Imagine that you go off and do whatever you normally do with the rest of the day. Then tonight, you fall asleep. Nothing unusual. But, while you're snoozing, a very strange and wonderful thing occurs.

The strange thing is that… a miracle happens!

This miracle is a very special one, tailored just to you. The miracle is that all the problems and concerns you have today are solved. Wonderful!

But the thing is, the miracle happened while you were asleep, so you don't know anything about it. When you wake up tomorrow, you are solidly in the world of the miracle, 24/7, but at first you are unaware that it has occurred.

So the question is: Tomorrow morning, from the moment you wake up and as you step through your first miraculous day, what do you notice—in yourself, in your surroundings, in other people—that eventually gets you scratching your head, thinking, "Something's different about today. A miracle must have happened!"

Asking this question takes you into new territory. There, you may encounter struggles you might not otherwise have had to go through. But it's also the first step to making this miracle your reality.

You can answer the question out loud with a friend, or you can describe the miracle day in writing.

Some questions to ask yourself, as you step through your first miracle day:

- How do I feel when I open my eyes on the first morning of my miracle life?

- Am I in the same bedroom? The same house? With the same people?

- What's different as I get ready for the day?

- What's different as I step through it, hour by hour?

- What do other people in my life notice about me that's different?

- What do I notice about them?

As you answer these questions, you gradually come to see that your problems are no longer your problems in this new life.

You're looking for a shift in perspective like Dorothy's after the tornado deposited her in Oz. Dorothy steps out of her house, looks around, and, as the film itself shifts from black and white to Technicolor, she sees the yellow brick road, the horse of many colors, the munchkins. She turns to her little dog and exclaims, "Toto, I've a feeling we're not in Kansas anymore!"

You're looking for that "I'm not in my old life anymore" moment.

You realize that this day is something new, something better, something that *feels* miraculous—but is also attainable. Then it's just a matter of working toward that "miracle," one doable step at a time.

The Miracle Question defines the goal, but getting there takes four additional steps:

1. **Scale.** After you have answered the Miracle Question, reflect on what pieces of the miracle are already part of your life, in whole or in part. Then evaluate where you are these days on a scale of 1–10, where "1" is how things were when they were as far away from the miracle as they have ever been in your adult life, and "10" is you're living the miracle 24/7. There are no right/wrong, good/bad numbers. The number you come up with is simply where your Miracle Question journey begins.

2. **Experiment.** Next, decide on an Experiment that you believe will move you closer to the miracle and that you can do in the coming week. The choice is important. Generally, what doesn't work is an Experiment you'd planned to do anyway, or one so daunting that you won't even attempt it. The best Experiment is something you really want to do, even if you feel some anxiety about it or you've been procrastinating. It's also important that just doing the Experiment, regardless of the outcome, will advance your score. Commit to doing the Experiment in the next week and estimate how much you believe it will move you toward a "10." For example, let's say you decide you're a 3.5 on the 1-10 scale right now and you estimate that when you do the Experiment, you'll be a 4. (For more on The Experiment, see Chapter 6.)

3. **Re-evaluate.** After the week has passed, look back at what happened. Did you do the Experiment? If so, how much did it actually advance your score? If you didn't do it, why not? Did

something get in the way? Or did you do something else that advanced your score, instead?

4. **Make course corrections.** After you re-evaluate, make course corrections as needed to refine the process. Then, re-scale, create a new Experiment, and, a week later, evaluate how that went. Continue to repeat this process until, week by week, month by month, you create the miracle you imagined—or something even better. Then, if you feel there's more you'd like to accomplish, ask the question again and get going on another miracle.

It's difficult to get somewhere if you don't know where you want to go or you don't have a way to check that you're on the right path. Answering the Miracle Question helps us envision the desired destination. The Experiments move us forward. And the 1–10 scaling lets us know if we're still on track.

Much as Dorothy discovered she always had a home, the Tin Woodman found his compassion, the Scarecrow displayed his brilliance, and the Cowardly Lion showed his courage, by traversing our own yellow brick roads, we become who we are meant to be.

Perhaps today is when you begin a journey down *your* yellow brick road. What will you notice when you wake up tomorrow in Oz?

5. Restore Balance

Security against defeat implies defensive tactics; ability to defeat the enemy means taking the offensive.

- **Sun Tzu**, *The Art of War*

In the assessment and planning stages, we learn about ourselves, our goals, our nemeses, and our allies. Then it's time to move from insight to action.

Insight is often helpful. It can identify the root of a problem, ferret out mistaken beliefs, make sense of missteps, and even point the way to new and better lives. But insight alone is seldom enough to effect lasting change. And, as one of my former professors once said, "Sometimes insight is the last defense."

Actions, we know, are more powerful than words.

The actions described in this chapter are designed to directly counteract UnBalancer's negative effects and lead the way back to balance.

For most of us, the best place to start rebalancing is with what we already know.

Whether UnBalancer has knocked us down with a sudden blow, worn us down with stress, or beaten us down with our demons, taking inventory of tactics and activities that have helped us before and incorporating them back into our routine is easier, quicker, and usually more efficient than learning entirely new strategies.

A Mini Lesson in Mini Self-Care

"But how can I do that," you might ask, "if I'm already too busy, too depressed, too stressed, too distracted (and so on) to take on one more thing?"

The answer is mini self-care.

How I discovered mini self-care

I stumbled onto mini self-care in the summer of 1980, a year after I'd moved out of New York City, where I'd struggled mightily to make a career as a writer.

The summer before, after two of my roommates were mugged and I narrowly escaped the knife myself, I left Brooklyn's Bedford-Stuyvesant for parts unknown.

I'd arrived in New York City five years earlier with two books, two cameras, and a knapsack full of clothes, but by the time I left Brooklyn, I'd accumulated a small U-Haul truck's worth of possessions.

With two Parisian friends, I loaded my collection of books, tools, photography equipment, furniture, and a Yamaha motorcycle into a rental truck. We drove across New York State to Buffalo, where I dropped everything off at my mother's house—including the Parisians, who were continuing their trek across America.

A few days later, I flew to London to begin a two-month trip through the UK and Europe, to be followed by a residence at an artist colony in Virginia, where I hoped to figure out where I'd settle next.

Two days before my return flight from Brussels, Belgium, the airline company I'd planned to take home went out of business. The next flight I could get a seat on was a week away, and I didn't have enough American Express Travelers Cheques left to buy another ticket.

But fear not! I'd worked my way through college and supported myself afterwards by doing a variety of construction jobs, and one of the trades I'd learned was roofing. And as luck would have it—or so I thought—the brother of the friend I was staying with was a roofer.

I'd sworn off construction work a couple of years before. Balancer was keeping an eye out for me, figuring I would end up missing a thumb or walking with a limp if I kept at it. But, Balancer be damned! This job was low stress and seemed like fun.

The Belgian materials and techniques were a little different from what I was used to, but within a few hours I was keeping up with the rest of the crew. I earned more than enough that week to pay for the flight home.

Three months later, toward the end of my stay at the Virginia artist colony, I was still unsure about where to go next. As luck would have it—or so I thought again—an opportunity popped up to extend my stay at the colony by helping to build new artist residences. This job, too, looked like fun. "Why not?" I thought.

Three weeks into it, I had my answer in the form of two ruptured disks.

My days of supporting myself with construction work were now behind me. I had to find another way to keep bread on the table.

ReBalancer kicked in and reminded me that I'd spent my childhood as a kid scientist, and that if push ever came to shove, I could work with computers. When I recovered enough from the back injury to become mobile again, I enrolled in a crash course in computer programming at Boston University.

And this is where mini self-care comes in.

The B.U. program crammed a six-course minor in Computer Science into one summer-long session. Course work that normally would have taken a semester was squeezed into seven days. Each evening was our "weekend," and each weekend was a virtual semester break. It was an intense, demanding educational experience unlike anything I'd ever encountered.

But the program came with unintended benefits. Besides learning the fundamentals of computer science, I stumbled on a new way to take care of myself.

To stay sane, I looked for small, quiet spaces in which to recover. I took short walks from the computer science buildings to the main campus, where for a few minutes I gazed out at the boats and ducks on the Charles River. I gave myself five-minute coffee breaks. I stuffed a paperback novel in my back pocket and read a few pages from it during lunch. Unlike my classmates who lived nearby and spent most of the night toiling at computer terminals in the lab, each evening I crossed the B.U. bridge back to Cambridge for a few hours of sleep and a brief return to normality.

Of the 24 students who began the program, I was one of only eight who completed it. I'm still convinced mini self-care was how I managed.

Mini self-care is the abridged version of full self-care.

We're wired to handle short-term stress. However, when stress goes on for too long, the constant flow of stress hormones takes a toll. If we reach a point where there's nothing left to give, we "burn out."

The optimal way to avoid burnout is to reduce the stress and weave back into our lives what we find restorative.

Many of us have evolved a set of activities that keep us feeling balanced and relaxed and help us to recuperate from stress. We might have a hobby, take trips or vacations, practice yoga, meditate, binge-watch a television series, hike, walk, swim, play a sport, garden, go for a ride, and so on. We do these things regardless of whatever else is going on in our lives, and they help to dissipate the tensions of work, health or family problems, financial stress—or even a bad winter.

But what can we do when we don't have time for any of that? When even half an hour of yoga or a 15-minute walk seems impossible?

The answer is still mini self-care!

Some examples:

Self-care: You do yoga for self-restoration.
Mini self-care: Pick one pose and do it for a couple of minutes, twice a day.

Self-care: You like to walk or run.
Mini self-care: Take a quick walk around the block.

Self-care: You like spending an hour at the end of the day reading.
Mini self-care: Carry a book with you and read a couple of pages at regular intervals.

Self-care: You like to talk with friends on the phone.
Mini self-care: Exchange short texts throughout the day.

Self-care: You take two-week vacations.
Mini self-care: Spend a night away on the weekend. If you can't take a night, walk downtown and pretend you're a tourist.

And so on.

Mini self-care isn't a permanent replacement for the full version, but many find it helpful not only in warding off burnout, but also as a first step toward a return to balance.

It helps us get into shape for full self-care when circumstances change.

What to do:

1. **Make a list** of the things you do that feel restorative.

2. **Figure out the shortest versions** that still feel meaningful. The 80/20 rule often applies: you can get 80% of the benefit from self-care activities by spending 20% of the time you'd really like to spend.

3. **Decide when to do your mini self-care.** Mini self-care is more effective if it's incorporated into a routine. Schedule some activities for morning, some at lunch, and others in the evening. Start with one or two mini self-care activities. Add additional ones only if you feel ready to do so.

4. **Add randomized mini self-care.** Try adding a mini self care activity you can do randomly throughout the day. For instance, get a meditation app that signals you to stop whatever you're doing and take three long, slow breaths—just long enough to get a fresh perspective. You can also stretch, go for a quick walk, drink a glass of water, or just zone out for a minute—whatever feels like self-care for you.

Mini self-care is a powerful ReBalancer tool, both in early stages of recovery from imbalance and as an UnBalancer repellent.

It's been a very long time since I last nailed down a shingle or wrote a line of computer code, but mini self-care continues to be a helpful rebalancing tool. Although I'm not as diligent as I could be about my morning, lunchtime, and evening mini self-care routines, when I practice them, body, mind, and spirit all hum along much more smoothly, regardless of the level or duration of stress.

Get a Flywheel, Become a Gyroscope

When UnBalancer topples us, mini self-care can get us functioning again. Once we're back on our feet, one of the best ways to stay vertical and unstuck, even in difficult times, is to access a **personal flywheel**.

A physical flywheel is a heavy disk that rotates evenly in response to repeated applications of kinetic energy. Flywheel-like disks show up in many places in the physical world. In a car, the flywheel transforms the jerky explosions of an internal combustion engine into vibration-free motion. A gyroscope is another kind of flywheel. You can push a spinning gyroscope in any direction and it will always right itself. Similarly, the mass of a potter's kick wheel translates periodic kicks into the steady rotation needed to create symmetrical bowls and platters.

A personal flywheel is an interest or passion that is not part of a job, a chore, or something to do for friends or family. It's an activity we do just for ourselves, independent of time, season, or circumstance.

Even when only intermittent energy is applied, a personal flywheel makes us more resistant to UnBalancer's sneaky moves.

Like a physical flywheel, a personal flywheel steadies us in the midst of difficulties, smoothing out the vibrations. No matter what's going on, somewhere inside us the wheel keeps spinning, spinning, and all we have to do is give it a little kick to keep it going. Then the flywheel's momentum keeps *us* going until we have a chance to catch our breath.

A personal flywheel can be anything you feel passionate about. For some it is a spiritual connection and the activities associated with it, whether they are participating in a religious community or observing their own private rituals. For many, it's doing something that feels creative, such as painting, writing, playing music, quilting, or other arts and crafts. For others, it's a physical activity—working out, doing yoga, playing a sport for the sheer joy of it. Outdoor activities such as gardening, hiking, boating, or fishing may also fill that role, as can a vast range of hobbies and avocations.

What is most important is that the activity be meaningful to you and that you do it, rain or shine, whether you are tired or full of energy, giving the wheel a little kick whenever you can to keep it spinning smoothly and your balance intact.

Getting the flywheel going, or bolting one on, is a ReBalancer activity, but once it's working, it becomes part of Balancer's stabilizing routine. (More on teaching Balancer some of ReBalancer's tricks in Chapter 7, "The Balancer/ReBalancer Loop.")

What to do:

1. **Make a list** of activities you used to like to do, still like to do today, or would like to do if time and money were no object.

2. **Circle the items** on the list that give you a feeling of interest, excitement, or curiosity.

3. **Pick one activity** that you would like to add back or, if it's new, to add to your life.

4. **Get started on it!** To make sure the flywheel keeps spinning, schedule it into your daily or weekly routine.

6. THE EXPERIMENT

Just as water retains no constant shape, so in warfare there are no constant conditions.

- **Sun Tzu**, *The Art of War*

"We've never seen anything like this!" shouts the General to his cadre in the crowded Situation Room.

An alien menace has humanity at its mercy! Nothing in our mighty arsenal can touch it! We'll be destroyed or dominated within days unless ...

... unless, as the story inevitably plays out, we apply Yankee ingenuity, uncover the invaders' vulnerabilities, and invent the means to exploit them.

The unknown enemy and the heroic victory against it has appeared in countless science fiction stories. The plot's turning point is always someone defying convention (and the General) and conducting an Experiment.

The Experiment is also, often, the key to our own victories against the depredations of UnBalancer.

We all began our lives as experimenters. *What happens if I close my hand around my foot and pull? What if I tug on my mother's hair? What if I stuff that into my mouth?* Beginning in infancy, Experiments are how we learn about ourselves, the world, and the way things work.

Unfortunately, like the hapless generals in science fiction stories, we often lose track of our experimental attitude as social conditioning insidiously snuffs it out.

Many of us learned to stop experimenting before we left elementary school. Instead of continuing our own explorations, we were taught to look to others or to existing methods for ways to deal with our problems.

Sometimes this tactic works fine—it's not always necessary to reinvent the wheel. But when existing solutions fail us, we need to learn how to experiment again.

ReBalancer and the Experiment

Most of the time, Balancer monitors our thoughts, feelings, and responses so we can maintain equilibrium. When this semi-automatic system can't deal with a situation, Balancer starts to tilt, and we tilt along with it. That's when ReBalancer kicks in.

ReBalancer is Balancer's Chief of Staff. When UnBalancer rages and Balancer tilts, klaxons sound—ReBalancer's cue to take over the helm.

But before ReBalancer can act, it has to determine what the problem is and whether it has the means to resolve it. The need for an Experiment arises when the problem is unfamiliar, or when there is no existing method to solve it.

ReBalancer goes through a decision tree:

1. **QUESTION**: Have I seen this problem before?

1. **IF YES, THEN**: Do I have a method to handle it?

2. **IF YES, THEN**: Use that method to beat back UnBalancer.

3. **OTHERWISE**: Gather data and conduct an Experiment.

The goals of ReBalancer's Experiments are similar to those of the scientist heroes of science fiction movies.

An Experiment provides new data. The new data generates insights into the nature of a problem, and from those insights come new potential solutions. How long it takes to solve the problem depends on the problem itself and on ReBalancer's skill in designing and implementing Experiments.

The Power of the Experiment

Without Experiments, ReBalancer is stuck in a loop, trying to solve new problems with old solutions—a formula for failure.

The Bill Murray film *Groundhog Day* is a textbook example of the power of the Experiment to break this cycle.

When the movie begins, Murray's arrogant weatherman character, Phil Connors, is eager to get together with his producer, Rita Hanson (played by Andie MacDowell), but he's far too much of a jerk for her to respond to his advances with anything but annoyance.

The morning after a day of filming Punxsutawney, PA, on Groundhog Day, Phil inexplicably wakes up to an exact repetition of the previous day. He's trapped in a time vortex, living February 2nd again and again.

Phil's fate seems sealed until, after reliving many duplicate Groundhog Days, he decides to conduct a series of Experiments. By applying what he's learned from previous repetitions, he starts to grow emotionally, becomes more aware of the needs of others, and works to improve the lives of Punxsutawney's citizens.

Many Experiments later, he's become someone worthy of Rita's attention. The next morning, he awakens on February 3rd, freed from his time loop, a transformed and more authentic version of himself. **Score: ReBalancer 1, UnBalancer 0.**

Another example comes from the annals of medicine.

For many decades, the medical establishment pushed the idea that stomach ulcers were caused by stress, spicy foods, and too much stomach acid. Ulcers were treated—ineffectively—with bland diets, antacids, and acid reducers.

In 1982, two Australian doctors hypothesized that ulcers were actually caused by the bacterium *H. pylori*.

Because an entrenched ulcer-medication industry was invested in the treatments of the day, these doctors (who years later were awarded the Nobel Prize for their discovery) couldn't get permission to test their hypothesis on patients. So one of them, Barry Marshall, conducted his own Experiment: He drank the contents of a Petri dish infected with *H. pylori*.

Within two weeks, Marshall developed severe gastritis, a precursor to ulcers. Then he quickly cured himself with antibiotics known to be effective against *H. pylori*.

Marshall's Experiment completely transformed ulcer management. Marshall later commented, "Everyone was against me, but I knew I was right." **Score: ReBalancer 1, UnBalancer 0.**

My own life has been a series of Experiments that shifted me in ways I needed to shift.

Sometimes an Experiment started something new. The Flower Mandalas that accompany my book *Paths to Wholeness: Fifty-Two Flower Mandalas*, for instance, began as an Experiment.

For several months I'd been using a photo editor to transform photos of clouds, rocks, wood, and other subjects into mandala-like images. Then one day, on the way home from a beach walk, I took a picture of a dandelion seed head.

A few days later, looking at the photo on my computer screen, I wondered what would happen if I "mandalaized" something that was already mandala-like. From this Experiment came my first Flower Mandala, the Flower Mandalas book, and the blossoming of a new way for me to see.

Experiments have also helped me overcome fear and expand my abilities. Sometimes these expansions have been specific to a particular situation, but often they have led to a more general, permanent change.

Here's the "before" and "after" of a recent Experiment in motorcycle maintenance:

Before the Experiment: In my 20s, motorcycle maintenance was an integral part of the motorcycling experience. When I returned to riding after a long hiatus, I wanted to recapture that aspect of motorcycling.

But my skills were as rusty as my 1972 Yamaha Twin. Simple tasks like changing the oil or cleaning the carburetor were scary, and when I encountered an unfamiliar problem, I often panicked. If something didn't work the first time, I'd repeat it with increasing force and a feeling of urgency, hoping against hope that what hadn't worked the first time would do the trick the second, third, or fourth. The net effect was broken parts, expensive repairs, and deepening discouragement. **Score: UnBalancer 1, ReBalancer 0.**

The Experiment: A valve-adjustment Experiment turned that around.

My bike's four valves needed adjusting every 5,000 miles. When I looked up the procedure in the repair manual, manipulating a feeler gauge, a wrench, and a screw driver in the cramped space available seemed daunting. ReBalancer kicked in and I asked my brother Mark for help.

Mark is a mechanical engineer and motorcycling instructor, and he has an engineer's confidence that if one person can design a piece of machinery, another can fix it.

On his first try, Mark couldn't get the feeler gauge in place. My body tensed up, ready to panic, but Mark just paused, thought about what he'd learned from this attempt, and then conducted an Experiment: He bent the feeler gauge so it more easily reached the gap.

This was better, but there was still a problem getting the wrench in place. So he stepped back again and designed a new Experiment, switching to an angled wrench. By the third Experiment, he got it, and he quickly adjusted the remaining valves.

After the Experiment: Since then, I've incorporated the Experiment into my own motorcycle maintenance practice, regaining not only the mechanical agility I thought I'd left behind, but also a deeper sense of self-confidence. **Score: ReBalancer 1, UnBalancer 0.**

The psychotherapy treatment room is a laboratory for Experiments.

I have witnessed many clients make Experiments that empower them to tackle the challenges they face. Clients ask: *What if I were to test this limit, take steps down that path, plunge into these waters?* Over time, they become emboldened to do what their parents, teachers, or peers had convinced them was impossible.

One young client detested writing assignments. He resisted writing because he believed his teacher wanted him to write about how much he "loved school," which he detested. To redirect his rage, we experimented with using irony and sarcasm. He was soon thrilled to discover that his teacher had no idea the conventional-seeming sentiments he was expressing were the opposite of what he really believed. **Score: ReBalancer 1, UnBalancer 0.**

An art student I worked with several years ago executed a more striking Experiment.

His life was fraught with addiction, depression, dysfunctional relationships, and a hostile and unsupportive family. He needed more help than he could get from counseling alone, but he'd learned from childhood experience not to ask for it.

So we devised an Experiment: At least once in the next week, he agreed to ask for help in a situation where normally he would have remained silent.

On a windy, bitterly cold afternoon a couple of days later, he stopped at a McDonald's for a hamburger and coffee. When he looked for somewhere to sit, he saw that all the tables were occupied. He buttoned up his thin winter coat and was about to eat his burger outside in the biting wind when he remembered the Experiment.

Instead of leaving with his food, he asked a young man sitting alone at a table for four if he could join him. The young man said "yes," and my client and he had a lively, animated lunch together.

This small Experiment was a turning point. My client realized not only that he could ask for help, but also that when he did, he was likely to get it.

Over the course of the school year, he received assistance and advice from several sources and was able to quit using drugs, leave a job where his coworkers expected him to be the "party boy," return to making art, and resolve major issues with his family. Even his lover quit drinking and drugging. **Score: ReBalancer 1, UnBalancer 0.**

Mistaken Beliefs and Experimental Attitudes

In the realm of personal transformation, Experiments are most useful when they test Mistaken Beliefs we hold about who we are and how we are permitted to interact. We form these beliefs when we're too young to know they may be inaccurate. They often work like a hypnotic spell, unconsciously limiting our actions as long as we remain under their influence.

Mistaken Beliefs are one of UnBalancer's basic resources for keeping us down. Unlike acute unbalancing events such as an accident, a major loss, or some other misfortune, Mistaken Beliefs act continuously, artificially dampening our potential, keeping us smaller than we need to be.

My artist client in the example above believed, mistakenly, that there was no point in asking for help. I believed, mistakenly, that if I couldn't solve a motorcycle problem on the first try, it was beyond my abilities. Bill Murray's weatherman character believed, mistakenly, that his arrogance and selfishness were appealing to women. In each of these situations, it was an Experiment that finally broke down the Mistaken Belief.

The Experiment is one of the most potent tools in ReBalancer's toolbox because it gives us the power to deal with the unknown. Unlike techniques and strategies to handle known challenges UnBalancer might throw at us, the Experiment enables ReBalancer to craft new strategies on the fly, expanding our personal universes.

These new strategies, once created, cannot be uncreated. They are always there, ready whenever we need them. And consistently doing Experiments leads to an experimental attitude, enabling us to feel confident that we can handle whatever unknowns our lives hand us with curiosity, resourcefulness, and equanimity.

The result is liberation.

Life itself becomes an ongoing Experiment. Instead of conforming to the limits of past patterns, we just *do*, see what happens, and adjust our view of reality accordingly, free from the manacles of Mistaken Beliefs.

What to do:

Like any experimenter, when our ReBalancers design Experiments, they follow a sequence of steps:

1. **Observe the current situation to see what needs to change.**
    Examples: **a)** My motorcycle's valves need adjustment or the engine will be damaged. **b)** Current ulcer treatments don't really work. **c)** My art student's life was in crisis.

2. **Develop a hypothesis about how to implement change**. Examples: **a)** If I use a system like my brother Mark did, maybe I can learn from failed attempts. **b)** Ulcers might be caused by a pathogen that can survive in stomach acid. **c)** If I ask for help, I may get it.

3. **Test the hypothesis with an Experiment**. Identify a small, experimental action that can test the hypothesis, where the success or failure of the action is not of crucial consequence, but the Experiment is still significant enough to bring all the relevant factors to bear. Examples: **a)** Bend a feeler gauge to reach the valve adjustment gap. **b)** Try infecting myself with H. pylori to see if it causes an ulcer. **c)** Ask a guy at McDonalds if I can share his table.

4. **Evaluate the outcome**. If things move in a desired direction, do more of what worked. If not, see what you can learn to better understand the problem, then design a new Experiment. Examples: **a)** Try the valve-adjustment approach on the other valves. **b)** See if antibiotics that cure gastritis can also cure ulcers. **c)** Ask for help again.

5. **Repeat steps 1 - 4 on an increasingly larger scale** until the new behavior is part of who you are, folded into your personal Balancer.

The best Experiments are typically ones we feel some anxiety about trying, or that we have been putting off, but which, when we do them, give us a sense of progress. They are large enough to matter, but not so daunting that they are too scary to attempt. And the very best are those that we feel good about doing regardless of the outcome.

When we're equipped with an experimental attitude, not even UnBalancer's invading aliens can defeat us.

PART III.
BALANCE MAINTAINED

He who can modify his tactics in relation to his opponent and thereby succeed in winning, may be called a heaven-born captain.

- **Sun Tzu**, *The Art of War*

7. THE BALANCER/REBALANCER LOOP

We are not fit to lead an army on the march unless we are familiar with the face of the country—its mountains and forests, its pitfalls and precipices, its marshes and swamps.

- **Sun Tzu**, *The Art of War*

We've seen how UnBalancer can knock us off kilter and how ReBalancer can swoop in to save the day, restoring Balancer's equilibrium—and our own. We'll learn more about strengthening Balancer in later chapters.

But first, let's take a birds-eye view of the whole cycle of Balance Lost, Balance Regained, and Balance Maintained.

Better to get the lay of the land before we head off on our mission.

Balancer Maintains Balance

Most of us stay balanced day to day because Balancer has learned three important things:

1. **What it feels like to be balanced.**

2. **What it feels like to lose balance.**

3. **What to do to restore balance.**

And most of the time, most of us cycle between being balanced, getting a little off balance, and recovering our balance again.

A simple example:

Let's say we usually wake up with good energy and positive motivation for the day. But one night, we toss and turn, fretting about the things we have to do in the days ahead, mentally tracking them all.

When we wake up the next morning, we feel as if we've worked all night. We're anxious, sluggish, exhausted, ill-equipped to manage the day ahead.

Let's say that from past experience, Balancer knows how to recover from a bad night. We take extra time during the day to meditate, walk, rest, or whatever we've learned helps us to reset ourselves. As a preventive measure, we also make a list of what we have to do the following day, so we don't have to lie awake trying to keep everything in our head. Then we go to sleep an hour early to make up for the restless night before.

By the following morning, balance is restored.

Balancer Unbalanced

But sometimes events in our lives or in the world seem to conspire to knock us over. UnBalancer gets the upper hand and Balancer can't cope. Or we're so caught up in what we're doing that we don't realize we've lost our equilibrium.

Maybe the stress builds up gradually. We have too much work, or not enough money, or we eat badly, or don't get enough sleep.

For a while, life moves along *almost* smoothly. Yes, we are a bit more tense, or crabby, or just don't feel right, but we're managing. We compensate for lack of sleep by drinking more coffee. We put off bill paying, or exercise, or other healthy aspects of our routine, figuring we can catch up later. We're still doing *okay*. But we've stopped taking the time to do what keeps us whole.

As the unbalancing process continues, more things start to go awry. A credit card company hits us with an overcharge. We start to show up late for work. We have a minor fender bender. Sleep increasingly eludes us.

To escape the stress, we lose ourselves in video games, the Internet, social media. We drink too much. But we can still pull ourselves together and get through the day. Most of the time.

Eventually, as the stresses slowly but surely accumulate, our coping mechanisms grow increasingly less responsive and our resilience erodes until finally, we tilt. We get sick. We have a major accident. A significant relationship starts to deteriorate, or it ends. We get fired. We can't pay the rent or the mortgage.

At this point, Balancer is in full tilt and UnBalancer is on top of the world.

Or maybe the stress comes not from a gradually decaying orbit but from an outside force. From out of nowhere, we get hit hard and don't have the inbuilt or learned capacity to deal with what's happened. Someone close to us dies unexpectedly. Our house burns down. We're seriously injured in an accident. We contract a major illness.

We never saw these things coming, and they lay us out flat.

Here, too, Balancer is on the ground and UnBalancer raises its fist in triumph.

For now.

ReBalancer to the Rescue!

But all is not lost!

Fortunately, Balancer's on-call Ally, ReBalancer, responds to the crisis.

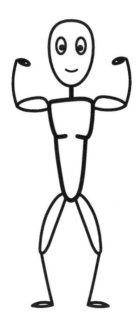

ReBalancer is the part of us that knows how to handle an emergency or, if it can't, is willing and able to figure it out.

When things go haywire, ReBalancer can assess the situation, determine how to stop the downward spiral, and begin the process of recovery.

Sometimes, ReBalancer reuses old techniques, but often it has to try new things on the fly or call in external support. Maybe it picks up self-soothing skills, or overcomes our resistance to asking for help, or finds an advocate to guide us through a complex medical system, or a financial one.

Whatever we need to rebalance, whenever possible, ReBalancer tries to get the job done, and when it's finished, it files away what it's learned for future use.

Balance Regained

At this point, Balancer's happy again, and so are we. And if we've played our cards right, we're stronger and more resilient than we were before, because we've incorporated what ReBalancer has mastered into our daily lives.

If we've played our cards right.

Balance Maintained

After we recover from an UnBalancer attack, we can't just stop at regaining balance. If we do, we're likely to get thrown the next time UnBalancer sneaks up on us in its crafty way or hits us with something hard.

However, when we incorporate, into Balancer's daily routine, what we've learned during our comeback, we become more resilient. As our new skills become habits, Balancer grows stronger and more able to automatically handle course corrections in the future.

For example, let's say that during a crisis, we've learned that exercise helps us feel more able to handle challenges. Afterwards, we make exercise part of our daily or weekly routine. Or let's say that during a crisis, we reached out to friends, family, and other supports. Once the crisis has passed, we still keep those connections active.

Balance is not only restored, but what ReBalancer has learned is permanently incorporated into our skill set. Then we monitor our equilibrium, detecting the early warning signs of a Balancer crash while it's still possible to prevent it, and we head UnBalancer off at the pass.

What to do:

1. **Make a list of the internal resources—the things you can do for yourself—that helped you regain balance.** List physical activities like working out at the gym or gardening, hobbies, creative projects, centering practices such as meditation or yoga, and anything else you did yourself that, when you were in an unbalanced state, helped you regain your equilibrium. The Circles of Problems and Resources tool might be a good memory jog. (See Chapter 4, "Assess and Plan.")

2. **Make a list of the external resources—the things you do with others—that helped you regain balance.** Include support groups, mentors, therapists, group activities, spiritual organizations, and any other ways you connected with others that, when you were unbalanced, helped you get back on your feet again. Here, too, the Circles of Problems and Resources tool is a helpful aid.

3. **Build these resources into your routine.** The things that helped you regain balance in the past will almost certainly help you again in the future.

By incorporating what helped you during a previous crisis into your daily or weekly routine, you equip Balancer to handle similar UnBalancer forces in the future.

Teaching Balancer the tactics that ReBalancer used to get you on your feet is essential. But, just as important for maintaining balance are Balancer-boosting strategies that can help anyone become more resilient.

Coming up next!

8. BUILD RESILIENCE

In all fighting, the direct method may be used for joining battle, but indirect methods will be needed in order to secure victory.

- **Sun Tzu**, *The Art of War*

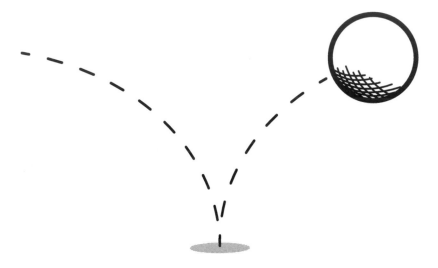

ReBalancer is "a friend in deed" when we're in need.

Think of ReBalancer as an emergency support. ReBalancer's job is to handle out-of-the-ordinary stresses and make us stable again. ReBalancer leaps into action when our default stabilizer, Balancer, gets thrown out of whack. But relying on ReBalancer alone to keep us on an even keel is a questionable strategy.

To reliably stay in balance, we need Balancer, our built-in self-correcting monitor, to be healthy, strong, and capable.

Balancer doesn't ask us for much. Much like our immune system, it chugs along on autopilot, making minor course corrections when needed. Only when it encounters something it can't handle does it call on ReBalancer for assistance.

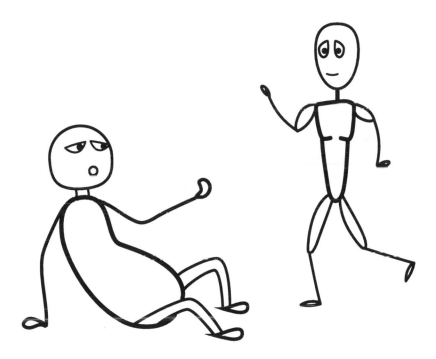

For most of us, most of the time, this Balancer/ReBalancer tag team works very well. But if Balancer is weakened through too much stress for too long, or was never very robust to begin with, we become much more vulnerable to UnBalancer.

Then, if Balancer is overwhelmed by a sudden stressor (an accident, a death, a financial crisis, etc.), it may crash before Re-Balancer can take over. Recovery from such crashes can take a long time, and if the crash is sufficiently severe, the damage can be permanent.

The key to building resilience and strengthening Balancer is not only to incorporate what ReBalancer does into Balancer's regular routine, but also to deliberately strengthen Balancer itself. Just as we can help our immune systems to better handle assaults to our bodies, we can better equip Balancer for handling whatever UnBalancer throws our way.

To do that, we need to build Resilience.

Resilience is the ability to bounce back. In a physical object, it is elasticity—the tendency of an object to return to its original shape after it's been deformed. In an ecosystem, it is the environment's capacity to rebuild itself. In a person, it is the ability to recover from shocks to our systems.

Without sufficient resilience, we are overcome by obstacles in our path. With it, nothing can keep us down.

Resilience in materials is intrinsic, but in people it's a dynamic quality. Like a muscle, resilience can be damaged by too much stress or can atrophy if neglected. But it also gets stronger with exercise.

Human resilience has two aspects: physical and psychological. Both are partly determined by nature, partly by nurture. Just as some people are born with greater resistance to disease, some of us show signs of greater psychological resilience even at very early ages. But the larger share of resilience is the product of our own efforts to build and maintain it.

In the Balancer/ReBalancer/UnBalancer framework, resilience is the property of Balancer that allows us to spontaneously recover from the negative effects of UnBalancer. Rather than calling in the troops for reinforcement, a resilient Balancer takes a momentary hit, adjusts to the impact, and bounces back, carrying us along with it.

When I was young, I was fascinated by the properties of natural and man-made materials. I still remember experimenting with the bounciness   the resilience   of round objects. I studied tennis balls, rubber balls, badminton balls, golf balls, glass marbles, ball bearings, always looking for something that could bounce higher than the last thing I tried. I ended this quest when I found, in the toy section of our local pharmacy, the Super Ball.

Super Balls, invented in 1964 by chemist Norman Stingley, are made from an amazingly elastic synthetic rubber called Zectron. When dropped, a Super Ball bounces nearly to the height from which it fell. When thrown down hard, it can easily bounce over a house.

In my therapy practice, I see many people whose resilience has been beaten down or in whom it was never sufficiently developed. They're like worn-out tennis balls. After we deal with the problems that brought them into therapy, much of our work together involves creating a more resilient approach to life, so they can transition from worn-out tennis balls to Super Balls.

These are the six main factors I've found that can build psychological resilience and keep Balancer on track:

1. **Creating** a resilience-friendly environment by reducing and managing stress

2. **Adopting** a growth-oriented attitude and a positive bias, rebalancing the brain

3. **Boosting** connections and supports

4. **Increasing** adaptability to change

5. **Practicing** balance-enhancing, mindful activities

6. **Monitoring** for signs of imbalance

Chapters 9-15 go into each of these factors. In them, you can learn how to build your own resilience to Super Ball capacity.

9. Manage and Reduce Stress

Ground on which we can only be saved from destruction by fighting without delay is desperate ground.

- **Sun Tzu**, *The Art of War*

Stress is one of the most insidious challenges to building resilience. It can be a constant strain on Balancer, gradually wearing down its efficacy and slowing its response time.

Basic ways to reduce stress that therapists often recommend include changing your emotional relationship to the stressor and practicing stress reduction techniques such as meditation or yoga. But the most effective method, if possible, is to remove or reduce the stressor itself.

The best place to start resilience-building is your environment.

Think about your home, your car, your job, your relationships. Focus on ways to reduce unnecessary stress. Anything that interferes with living a peaceful life is a candidate for stress-reducing changes.

You can often completely eliminate minor stressors that add emotional noise. Things like sharpening dull kitchen knives, creating a system so you don't misplace your keys, replacing a cell phone that keeps losing its charge, or changing your route to work might seem small, but the toll these stressors take is cumulative.

More challenging stressors like ending a toxic relationship or transitioning from the wrong job or career are, of course, harder to eliminate, but making those changes can create a huge boost to resilience.

Regardless of the source of stress, the first question to ask yourself is, "Can this change?" and if the answer is "yes," change it!

I encountered a striking example of the efficiency and effectiveness of removing a stressor several years ago. I was working with a bright, affable 12-year-old boy who, despite an obvious interest in learning, was always getting suspended from school. When I asked him about the events that led to his suspensions, I noticed that he always smiled when he talked about getting his teachers angry.

I visited his home and discovered that he had an angry and imposing stepfather. Provoking his teachers was my young client's way of dealing with his resentment toward his stepfather—he could enrage his teachers and they wouldn't hit him, but his stepfather might.

A typical intervention in cases like this is family therapy, so with the family's permission I returned a week later. My client lived in a house adjacent to his mother's business, and there was a constant interchange between the two locations, affecting all members of the family in some way.

During the session, I asked each family member to imagine what their lives would be like if they woke up the next day and all their problems were solved. The first thing each one said—even the five-year-old—was that they'd be living somewhere else.

A month later, they moved, and very soon afterward, my 12-year-old client stopped acting out in school.

Clean up the cat hairs!

A related aspect of creating a safe, resilience-friendly environment involves "**cat hairs.**" When you find yourself overreacting to a comment, a tone of voice, or a situation, or you inexplicably feel sad, angry, jealous, or some other difficult emotion, you might have a problem with cat hairs.

Of course, I don't mean literal cat hairs. I love cats!

The term "cat hair," in this context, comes from an experiment with lab rats.

Researchers wanted to see if rats are genetically programmed to fear cats. They placed several rat pups who had been exposed only to people and other rats—never to a cat—in a cage and monitored their playfulness for several days.

The rats played together freely until, on the fourth day, the researchers took the smallest cat stimulus they could think of, a *single cat hair*, and dropped it into the center of the cage. Soon, the pups stopped playing and ran to the edges of the cage, trembling with fear.

After 24 hours, the researchers removed the cat hair. They continued monitoring the rat pups, but days later, the rats had not returned to their baseline playfulness. Where there had once been a cat hair, the pups seemed to fear, there might still be a cat.

Fear and trauma can leave an indelible imprint on us, too.

Our automatic fear-handling mechanism makes us prone to reacting to our "cat hairs" with fight/flight/freeze responses. Such triggered reactions can negatively affect our jobs, relationships, and many other aspects of our lives, cheating us out of a more full version of ourselves.

Fortunately, humans have more options than rats do for dealing with "cat hairs."

Reminders of traumatic experiences that trigger strong emotions can often be removed. Sometimes these are physical objects, but more often they are habitual actions. For example, if a certain phrase or tone spoken by a friend, relative, or romantic partner reminds you of a bad relationship or a difficult childhood, you can ask him or her to change it. Most people will comply with a request like this when it's presented in context.

When cat hairs can't be removed, we can learn to see them merely as hairs.

If your emotional response seems stronger than the situation merits, ask yourself what triggered it. Did the trigger really mean what you felt it did, or did it just stir something inside?

Over time, as we come to understand that some triggers are just triggers, they gradually become less threatening. They're not cats, we see, but are merely cat hairs. Then we can use our fight/flight/freeze mechanism to protect ourselves from real threats, rather than reacting to cat hairs.

What to do:

1. **Notice** what is causing increased stress or a triggered response. Simply paying attention to the feeling and looking at what caused it often provides some relief.

2. **Remove** the stressor, when possible.

3. **Change your relationship** to stressors that can't be removed. For most of us, our attitudes toward stressors and the emotional responses those attitudes generate are more than half of the stress. Even triggered responses can be detoxified by changing our relationship to them.

4. **Accompany** the stress or triggered response. Learn to sit with the feeling rather than reacting to it or pushing it away. Feelings that are pushed aside tend to stay stuck, petrified within us like an ant in amber. Feelings that are reacted to tend to be reinforced. But when feelings are fully experienced, they can shift into different feelings. Fear can turn into peacefulness. Sadness can turn into acceptance. Anger can turn into understanding. Envy can become motivation.

5. **Develop self soothing skills.** When we are able to self-soothe, sometimes even the cat becomes just a kitten, purring on our laps. (More on self-soothing in Chapter 12, "Embrace Change.")

10. Rebalance Your Brain

The expert in battle moves the enemy, and is not moved by him.
- **Sun Tzu**, *The Art of War*

One of the most powerful resilience-building, Balancer-enhancing strategies is to consciously look for **growth opportunities** in experiences—to seek the silver lining in the cloud.

Looking for the growth opportunity in the struggle makes it possible for us to find it.

When we go through difficult times asking questions like, "What can I learn from this?" and "How can going through this make me a better person?" we gain leverage on our problems, and it becomes much harder for UnBalancer to unseat us. Instead of being knocked off course, we see obstacles as challenges and grow more resilient by overcoming them.

Difficulties become, as a friend of mine puts it, "just an **AFGO**— Another **F***ing Growth Opportunity**." Thinking of struggles as AFGOs allows us to accept, in a tongue-in-cheek but still meaningful way, that positive change can emerge from negative experiences.

Brain balancing and negative bias

A close cousin of the AFGO is learning to condition our minds to diversify. Though we are hard-wired to pay more attention to negative events, we can retrain ourselves to give equal attention to the positive.

Negative stimuli have about 20x greater impact than positive ones.

This is because our brains have evolved to contain twice as many cells that respond to threats as they do cells that process positive experiences, and these threat-detecting cells respond about 10 times as quickly. And because powerful experiences form stronger memories, the constant repetition of stronger responses and more vivid memories creates a cycle that reinforces a **negative bias.**

Our negative bias was once essential for survival.

All protohumans could safely eat something that tasted good and could ignore the movements of familiar creatures. But if something tasted rotten, only those who immediately spit it out were likely to avoid food poisoning, and only those who responded swiftly to a rustling in the brush escaped being eaten by predators.

Our negatively biased early ancestors survived to produce offspring, while those who failed to react quickly enough to possible threats didn't make it.

Modern brains respond similarly to those of our ancestors. We, too, immediately sense when something tastes off, but we can eat an entire meal without even realizing we've consumed it. And we, too, react quickly to our large, modern-day predators—other drivers and their vehicles—but can miss a turnpike exit when we're lost in thought or absorbed in music or conversation.

If this negative bias were limited only to quick responses to actual threats, it would still be a useful aid to survival. The problem is that our negative bias also makes it harder to fully take in and enjoy the positive aspects of our much safer world.

If a toe hurts, we may not notice that we are otherwise healthy. If we suffer a loss, we can lose track not only of all we still have, but also of what we are continuing to receive.

Our hard-wired, "better safe than sorry" bias often contributes to low-level pessimism. Even when things are going well, we may think, "Things are okay now, but wait until the other shoe drops."

To **recalibrate our brains**, we need to update our programming to take into account the relative safety of our present surroundings. By training ourselves to pay as much attention to the positives as we do to the negatives, we can rewire the brain to have a more positive, and more satisfying, bias.

The difference between a negative and a more balanced bias came to me most clearly during a brief conversation with one of the monks who led a Buddhist retreat I went to many years ago.

We sat together on a hillside overlooking the dining hall and ate our lunches while I talked with him about feelings of hurt, betrayal, and despair that followed the difficult ending of a long relationship. My UnBalancer was having a field day with the attention I'd been giving to the hurt and resentment these events had caused.

"I understand your feelings," the young monk said, "but this way of looking at love is too limited. You think it comes only from these people, and now it is gone. But love comes from many places."

He held out his sandwich. "The baker who made this bread shows us love. Yes, it is his business, but the bread is very good and there is love in it. And there are the trees and the grass. They give us oxygen—without them we could not live." He looked up at the sky. "And the sun gives us warmth."

As he continued to point out human and non-human sources of love, I felt a shift inside. Until that moment, the idea that "the universe loves us" had seemed so abstract it was meaningless. But now, listening to this young man as he took in the love of the cosmos, I vicariously experienced his gratitude, and I carry these feelings with me to this day.

Because it goes against the grain of our innate wiring, watering the seeds of a more balanced bias takes work—but it's worth the effort.

Simple everyday practices can help. We can start to focus only on eating our food instead of looking at social media or the newspaper at breakfast. On a road trip or commute, we can turn off the radio or smartphone and experience the world we're passing through. We can pause long enough, when we receive a compliment, to let that positive feedback settle into our being.

Small changes such as these help us to move beyond the programming that helped our ancestors survive their more hazardous world so that we can thrive in the one we live in now.

For more practices aimed at updating our programming, see Rick Hanson's book *Buddha's Brain: The Practical Neuroscience of Happiness, Love, and Wisdom.*

What to do:

1. **Smell the roses. Eat the raisin.** Literally. Negative stimuli hit us 10 times as quickly and twice as hard as positive ones. To even things out, take the time to fully absorb what tastes or smells good, feels nice, or sounds pleasing. Literally take in the smells of flowers, fragrances, foods. Enjoy the sound of a friend's laughter. Feel the textures of the objects you touch throughout the day—a partner's skin, the glassy screen of your smartphone, your own hair.

   An exercise: Eat a single raisin as slowly as you can. Feel its texture, notice its color, smell its scent, and chew it slowly until it liquefies, savoring its unique flavor and mouth feel. Then try this exercise again, but with something from your refrigerator.

2. **Look for the growth opportunities in everything.** See difficulties as teachers. The path from victim to victor is through seeking out and embracing opportunities for growth. Whether we like it or not, all difficult experiences really can be AFGOs.

   Develop the habit of seeing the growth opportunities in everything that comes your way. Crazy traffic on the commute to work? A learning opportunity for patience. An illness that could be serious? An opportunity to learn to deal with uncertainty. An annoying co-worker who can't stop talking? Another opportunity for learning patience—or for honing your assertiveness skills. And so on, with experiences from the most trivial to the most challenging.

3. **Create gratitude lists.** Frequently. Grateful people are generally more satisfied with their lives and relationships, cope better with difficulties, and are more generous, empathetic, and self-accepting.

A simple but effective tool for promoting a grateful perspective is the gratitude list. It's a way to reinforce the reality that whatever we may lack, we also have many things for which to be grateful. We may not have all the wealth we want, the health we want, the relationships we want, the things we want, but when we list what we do have, we have a lot.

When you make a gratitude list, be open to including anything at all that you feel grateful for. A 50-item gratitude list I created for a chapter in my book *Paths to Wholeness* starts with "Being alive" and ends with "Popsicles!"

11. Build Connections and Support

The good fighters of old first put themselves beyond the possibility of defeat, and then waited for an opportunity of defeating the enemy.
- **Sun Tzu**, *The Art of War*

For most of us, UnBalancer flourishes when we're isolated. We are social animals, and separation from others weakens our ability not only to thrive, but sometimes even to survive.

Ostracism—being ignored and excluded—threatens our basic need for belonging.

In other mammals, being ostracized cuts the individual off from the protection of the pack. The result is often death from predators or starvation. Human beings, too, are hard-wired to fear ostracism. In game-based experiments where participants' avatars are rejected by other players, the experimental subjects feel anxiety and depression *even when they know* that the other avatars are just computer simulations.

Establishing and maintaining close relationships, on the other hand, makes us more resilient.

A network of connections—friendships, family, support groups, spiritual groups, and group activities that validate our interests and identities—not only enriches our day-to-day lives, it also keeps us steady when the going gets tough. It's as if each connection is a guy wire, bracing us when UnBalancer huffs and puffs.

However, connections are not just a numbers game. It's important that our relationships are actually supportive. For many of us, that's a no-brainer. But for others, a crucial component of building a more resilient environment is discerning who, in our circles of friends, family, and associates, is an ally of our true selves, and who may actually be an ally of UnBalancer.

Those of us who grew up with strong social supports and positive mirroring of who we are tend to recreate positive-reinforcing relationships throughout our teenage and adult years. We automatically gravitate toward friends and romantic partners who are reciprocal in their relationships with us, and we feel buoyed up by our affinity groups.

But those of us who grew up with dysfunction in our relationships with family or friends may subtly replicate this dysfunction in later relationships. Instead of being surrounded by people who accurately mirrored who we were as individuals and in relationship to others, our views of ourselves were shaped by circus mirrors. This distorted mirroring can unconsciously shape our later connections.

For example, people who grow up with a narcissistic parent who offers only conditional love may choose narcissistic friends, employers, or romantic partners who leave them feeling "never good enough" no matter how hard they try. Or they may become "people pleasers," always doing for others but seldom letting others know what they, themselves, need.

Those who grow up isolated from their peers due to prejudice, economic disadvantage, temperament, or other differences often come to see themselves as "outsiders." Later in life, they may still find it hard to integrate themselves into groups.

Awareness is key to changing these patterns.

As we grow aware that we're repeating old, dysfunctional patterns, we begin to discover new, more functional ways to see ourselves and to relate to others. We assert our needs more directly, set our boundaries more explicitly, and reconsider the benefits and costs of keeping some of our friendships and family connections.

We grow more skillful at discerning life-affirming relationships, and we find ourselves naturally building new relationships with people who support our true selves.

What to do:

1. **Get rid of the crazy makers in your life.** Notice whether some of the people you've surrounded yourself with are more of a drain than they are a support. See if you can shift the balance, and if you can't, consider distancing yourself from these relationships.

2. **Water the seeds of connection.** We all get busy, but a quick text, email, or phone call keeps the lines of connection open and increases the pull of nurturing, face-to-face reunions with friends and family.

3. **Reevaluate people who are on the sidelines**, but who possess a generous, helpful nature. See if you can deepen these relationships. Arrange to spend more time together to explore the potential of these connections.

4. **Participate in activities you enjoy doing**. Current friends not interested in the things you love? Head out on your own, and open yourself to meeting new people who share your interests. Meetup.com groups, spiritual communities such as churches and temples, and recreational groups all provide opportunities for expanding connection.

    Look into physical fitness classes or day trips sponsored by town recreation departments or community centers. Take a cooking class at the local Adult Education organization. Check out lectures and presentations at public libraries or community colleges in your own or surrounding towns. Join a camera club. Choose activities that you'll enjoy on your own but may also attract like-minded, like-spirited potential friends.

5. **Create affinity groups.** Can't find a group that's doing something you'd rather not do alone? Create one! Reach out to your friends and social media contacts and see who else shares your interest, or start a Meetup.com group of your own.

    Anything goes! One friend mentioned his interest in poker on his Facebook page and several people outside his inner circle responded with enthusiasm, whether or not they had played the game before. Another started a monthly "gaming night." I began an artist group that's still running strong.

    The next step is easy—schedule a time, a place, and bring a snack. You only need a few participants to form a core group.

12. Embrace Change

By the laws of war, better than defeating a country by fire and the sword, is to take it without strife.

- **Sun Tzu**, *The Art of War*

Emotional adaptability is what helps us respond to changing circumstances and events without being unduly shaken by them. It's a Balancer characteristic and a key component of resilience.

People who are emotionally adaptable can bend with the wind, like saplings. Those who are less adaptable are likely to strain and crack as they struggle to maintain equilibrium.

Emotional adaptability varies from person to person and can also be impacted by life events. Most of us are less emotionally adaptable when we're under constant or unusual stress. Being attached to expectations of ourselves, others, or how things ought to be also limits emotional adaptability. Those of us raised in a rigid environment, with fixed ideas of how we or the world works, may also be less adaptable.

The good news is that there are many ways to become more adept at responding to change.

Some of the best strategies for enhancing emotional adaptability include practices that promote an accepting attitude, increase compassion and self-compassion, and enable forgiveness and self-forgiveness. Creative activities and an experimental attitude also increase our adaptability to change.

We'll delve into all of them in this chapter.

Radical Acceptance

For many of us, the biggest obstacle to emotional adaptability is not accepting things as they are.

When we resist accepting the true nature of ourselves and our surroundings, we live in a false reality that we must constantly defend against the evidence. We may worry excessively that our futures won't turn out the way we hope, or get stuck in the past, consumed by resentments over things not turning out how we wanted them to. We have fewer resources to deal with what's happening in the present and can't easily go with the flow or see the humor in our own situations.

Without acceptance, there can be little or no forward movement. We grow older, and the external circumstances of our lives continue to change, but we can't embrace them. As the rock group

Talking Heads put it, inside our heads it's "the same as it ever was, same as it ever was, same as it ever was."

As a way to open ourselves to how things really are, writer and teacher Tara Brach recommends practicing what she calls **Radical Acceptance**.

Radical acceptance means fully accepting our situations, feelings, limitations, and strengths. It's a prerequisite to meaningful change. Tara Brach explains, "When we can meet our experience with Radical Acceptance, we discover the wholeness, wisdom and love that are our deepest nature."

When we accept things as they are, we don't have to struggle against them. We can radically accept our bodies, our pasts, our peers, our partners, our children, and the strengths and limitations of our own personalities, and then we can move forward, changing what can be changed and embracing what cannot. As pioneering psychologist Carl Rogers observed, "The curious paradox is that when I accept myself just as I am, then I can change."

Radical acceptance can be as complex as accepting a traumatic loss or catastrophic event, or as simple as accepting the weather.

An example:

I've lived in the U.S. Northeast most of my life. Here, the winters can be harsh. I have never liked cold weather or snow, and I've never been drawn to winter sports. Each year, as the days shorten and the nights grow longer, I've felt a sense of dread as winter approaches, and a great sense of relief when I finally put away the snow shovel and hang up my winter coat.

But one year, winter just *was*. Autumn flowed into winter as it always does, and this time I was fine with it.

The weather acceptance switch had flipped the previous summer, during a meeting of the Buddhist study group I belong to. On an extraordinarily hot and humid evening, as we began our walking meditation, I was struggling with the discomfort of my shirt sticking to my back and the sweat beading on my forehead. Then our teacher said, "This is heat."

As we walked in silence, I pondered his observation, feeling into the reality of the present moment. Something shifted inside.

The rest of that evening, and for all the other hot days that summer, heat was simply heat, not something to be dreaded or avoided. When the cold set in again, I thought, "This is cold." When the snow fell, "This is snow." When it melted, "This is spring." And as the summer heat approached again, I remembered, "This is heat."

Radical acceptance is a balm for difficult emotions such as envy, resentment, and frustration. We accept our present circumstances and what has led up to them, and we understand that railing against them won't change anything.

Radical acceptance is also an antidote to the lingering pain of misfortune. When we radically accept our losses, we are more open to the possible gains that may come from them. Then we can move on, recovered.

When we radically accept something, we don't judge it. We don't get angry, we don't try to fight it, and we don't resent it. We simply recognize that this is how it is, freeing up all the energy we might otherwise have expended on judging, fighting, anger, or resentment. Then we can take in, with renewed openness, whatever comes our way.

What to do:

The following practice is one I've adapted from the many helpful guided meditations on Radical Acceptance in Tara Brach's book *Radical Acceptance: Embracing Your Life With the Heart of a Buddha*. Tara's website tarabrach.com also has many useful resources on Radical Acceptance, including guided meditations, articles, and courses. I encourage you to explore both the book and the website.

To do the practice:

1. **Sit in a comfortable, balanced position and close your eyes.** Notice the structures supporting you and relax into them. Pay attention to the rhythm of your breath as it enters your body, fills your lungs, and exits.

2. **Remember a situation that brings up feelings of anger, fear, envy, grief, or some other difficult emotion.** See the situation in your mind's eye. Hear, in your mind's ear, any words that were said. Notice, in your body, any sensations that come up as you recall this situation, paying special attention to your throat, chest, and stomach. Notice any other emotions that may arise. Let yourself feel all these emotions and sensations.

3. **Notice what happens when you resist the experience.** While you are seeing, hearing, and feeling the situation, imagine creating a powerful stream of "no" and using it to push the situation away. Notice how much effort it takes to keep pushing. Imagine how much more effort it will take to continue to push as you move through time in the days, weeks, months, and years ahead. Feel the weight of this accumulated effort in your body. This is the cost of resistance.

4. **Return your attention to your breath.** Notice the air entering your body, filling your lungs, and then leaving your body. With each breath, allow the stream of "no" to subside and its weight to dissipate. Sense the shift in your body as you let this resistance go. Then recall, again, the difficult situation from Step 2, once again letting yourself fully see, hear, and feel it in your body.

5. **Notice what happens when you radically accept the experience by saying "yes."** While you are feeling the emotions and sensations of the difficult situation, imagine creating

a powerful stream of "yes" that draws the feeling into your heart. Embrace the feeling as you would a child who needs your attention and comfort. Say "yes" to the difficult feeling, and also say "yes" to the part of yourself that wants to push it away. This part, too, needs your loving embrace.

6. **Notice any changes in your body as you continue to draw the difficult feeling into your embrace with the steady stream of "yes."** Do you sense a shift? A relaxation? Let yourself imagine the cumulative effects of saying "yes" if you continue to embrace the feeling in the days, weeks, months, and years ahead. This is the healing power of acceptance.

7. **Return your attention to your breath.** Notice, again, the rhythm of breath entering your body, expanding your lungs, and leaving your body. Let yourself acknowledge what you have gained from this meditation. Set an intention to say "yes" to whatever comes. Then open your eyes.

Compassion and Self-Compassion

Like Radical Acceptance, having a compassionate attitude toward ourselves and others promotes emotional adaptability. No longer burdened by self-criticism or perfectionistic standards, our internal Balancer is free to respond adeptly to our present reality.

Self-compassion is a term coined by researcher and psychologist Kristin Neff to describe extending to yourself the compassion you would feel for a good friend or someone you love.

When you feel compassion for others, Kristin explains, you are aware of their suffering and are moved by their pain. Rather than judging or criticizing them, you feel a strong desire to help. You approach them with kindness, offer support, and try to relieve their pain. You sympathize, recognizing that misfortune is part of the larger human experience and that nobody is completely spared from suffering.

"Having compassion for oneself is really no different than having compassion for others," Kristin says. "Self-compassion involves acting the same way towards yourself when you are having a difficult time, fail, or notice something you don't like about yourself. Instead of just ignoring your pain with a 'stiff upper lip' mentality, you stop to tell yourself 'this is really difficult right now,' how can I comfort and care for myself in this moment?"

Self-compassion is one of the most powerful tools for reducing critical self-talk and boosting self-esteem.

When we are compassionate toward ourselves, we don't give ourselves a hard time and we don't push our vulnerable feelings aside and "suck it up." Instead, we treat our difficult emotions as if they were a baby crying inside us and do whatever it takes to attend to them.

Practicing self-compassion helps us become more responsive not only to our own needs, but also to the needs of others. Released from the tyranny of our inner critics, we become more able to blossom into our full selves and, consequently, less self centered and more compassionate toward others.

We have more of ourselves to give away.

Extending compassion to others also makes us more resilient.

Giving to others lets us become our best selves, even when we feel depleted. This principle underlies healing practices in many indigenous cultures, where the shaman chooses a sickly boy to become his apprentice. The boy becomes strong through healing his people, but he must continue to heal others in order to stay healthy himself.

In my work as a psychotherapist, I have found this healing/healer link also to be true. Regardless of what is going on in my life, when I get to my office and put on my imaginary "therapist jacket," I become my best self, doing what I can to attend to the needs of my clients. Because I have been that best self all day, by evening the troubles of the morning have become smaller and more manageable. And the next day, I often awaken a little more emotionally adaptable, not only for my clients, but also for myself.

Kristin's website self-compassion.org includes a quick test to determine your level of self-compassion, as well as a series of practices and meditations that help to increase it. I encourage you to explore the website and to read her book *Self-Compassion: The Proven Power of Being Kind to Yourself.*

What to do:

The following practice is one I've adapted from the "Self-Compassion Break" exercise Kristin teaches. You can do this any time you feel unsettled, whenever you have a hurt that is unresolved, or simply as a way to experience self-compassion.

To do the practice:

1. **Recall a difficult or stressful situation in your life.** Let yourself feel where, in your body, you still hold the stress and discomfort. Pay particular attention to your throat, chest, and stomach.

2. **Find the place in your body that hurts and put your hands on it.** Sense into the hurting part. Experiment with moving your hands until they locate the area that hurts. Let your hands bring soothing warmth to this part of your body.

3. **Acknowledge this moment of suffering** by saying something like, "This hurts," or "This is stressful," or simply, "This is a moment of suffering."

4. **Acknowledge that suffering is a part of life.** Say to yourself something like, "Other people also feel suffering," or "Everyone has struggles," or simply, "Suffering is a part of life."

5. **Express kindness to yourself.** Find a phrase that the hurt part of you responds to. Phrases such as "I forgive you," "I love you," "I accept you," and "I appreciate you" are some examples, but each hurt part has its own special need. Experiment until you feel a shift in the part that hurts, a softening or relaxing.

6. **Let yourself feel the warmth of your touch and the compassion emanating from your heart.** Take time to let the hurt part absorb this warmth and compassion. Then, when you are ready, open your eyes.

Forgiveness and Self-Forgiveness

Like radical acceptance and self-compassion, the ability to forgive ourselves and others can free us from what Romantic poet William Blake called "mind-forged manacles"—in this case, feelings such as anger, hatred, resentment, guilt, shame, and victimization. Liberation from these feelings through forgiveness can help us be more available in the present moment and its ever-changing conditions.

Forgiveness, however, is sometimes difficult to achieve.

Some obstacles to forgiving are easy to understand. Forgiveness is hardest when there is ongoing harm. Before we can offer forgiveness, we must be safe; before we can ask to be forgiven, we must stop doing harm. Forgiveness is also challenging when injuries haven't healed. Unhealed wounds can lock us into a pattern of attracting others who may hurt us again, or they can imprison us in a self-protective shell that not only keeps out potential harm, but also healing.

But for many of us, the chief impediment to forgiveness is unwillingness.

Our culture glorifies an "eye for an eye and a tooth for a tooth" tradition that spans millennia. Forgiveness—forgiving others, seeking forgiveness, even forgiving ourselves—is seen as weakness. If we have been hurt, we may feel that we *should* punish those who harmed us, and if we cannot, we should at least punish them in our hearts. If we have harmed others, we may feel that we *should* punish ourselves, hoping that self-punishment will prevent us from harming again.

Releasing ourselves from these vengeful emotions through forgiveness may seem unfamiliar and unsafe. But refusing to forgive ourselves doesn't guarantee we will not harm again, nor does refusing to forgive others punish those who have harmed us. Withholding forgiveness merely uses up energy that could be put to more life-affirming purposes.

Sometimes forgiveness happens spontaneously. A personal example: Forgiving my father for our lifelong estrangement began with a dream I had several years after his death and concluded when I realized, finally, that I was no longer afflicted by what had been damaging in our relationship. I could then regard him with compassion, understand how his difficulties and limitations had shaped him, and forgive him for his part in our conflicts— and myself, for mine, lightening the load I had been carrying for decades.

More often, forgiveness is a process that can be helped along by conscious actions.

The most helpful tool I've encountered for fostering forgiveness is a Buddhist meditation popularized by psychologist and teacher Jack Kornfield. Within the safety of the meditation, it instructs us first to feel the pain of keeping our hearts closed and then offers gentle steps for opening them just enough to ask for forgiveness from those we have harmed, to forgive ourselves, and to forgive those who have harmed us. Cautioning that forgiveness may come slowly and cannot be forced, the meditation encourages a gradual letting go of the burdens of unforgiven acts, with each iteration lightening our load just a little, like a sigh of relief.

The following is Jack's version of the Forgiveness Meditation practice, as presented on his website jackkornfield.com. (You can also hear him reciting it on YouTube. Search for "Jack Kornfield self-forgiveness.")

What to do:

1. **Prepare for the forgiveness meditation.** To practice forgiveness meditation, let yourself sit comfortably, allowing your eyes to close and your breath to be natural and easy. Let your body and mind relax. Breathing gently into the area of your heart, let yourself feel all the barriers you have erected and the emotions that you have carried because you have not forgiven—not forgiven yourself, not forgiven others. Let yourself feel the pain of keeping your heart closed. Then, breathing softly, begin asking and extending forgiveness, reciting the following words, letting the images and feelings that come up grow deeper as you repeat them.

2. **Ask forgiveness from those you have hurt or harmed.** *There are many ways that I have hurt and harmed others, have betrayed or abandoned them, caused them suffering, knowingly or unknowingly, out of my pain, fear, anger, and confusion.* Let yourself remember and visualize the ways you have hurt others. See and feel the pain you have caused out of your own fear and confusion. Feel your own sorrow and regret. Sense that finally you can release this burden and ask for forgiveness. Picture each memory that still burdens your heart. And then to each person in your mind repeat: *I ask for your forgiveness, I ask for your forgiveness.*

3. **Offer forgiveness for yourself.** *There are many ways that I have hurt and harmed myself. I have betrayed or abandoned myself many times through thought, word, or deed, knowingly or unknowingly.* Feel your own precious body and life. Let yourself see the ways you have hurt or harmed yourself. Picture them, remember them. Feel the sorrow you have carried from this and sense that you can release these burdens. Extend forgiveness for each of them, one by one. Repeat to yourself: *For the ways I have hurt myself through action or inaction, out of fear, pain, and confusion, I now extend a full and heartfelt forgiveness. I forgive myself, I forgive myself.*

4. **Offer forgiveness for those who have hurt or harmed you.** *There are many ways that I have been harmed by others, abused or abandoned, knowingly or unknowingly, in thought, word, or deed.* Let yourself picture and remember these many ways. Feel the sorrow you have carried from this past and sense that you can release this burden of pain by extending forgiveness when your heart is ready. Now say to yourself: *I now remember the many ways others have hurt or harmed me, wounded me, out of fear, pain, confusion, and anger. I have carried this pain in my heart too long. To the extent that I am ready, I offer them forgiveness. To those who have caused me harm, I offer my forgiveness, I forgive you.*

5. **Let yourself gently repeat these three directions for forgiveness until you feel a release in your heart.** For some great pains you may not feel a release but only the burden and the anguish or anger you have held. Touch this softly. Be forgiving of yourself for not being ready to let go and move on. Forgiveness cannot be forced; it cannot be artificial. Simply continue the practice and let the words and images work gradually in their own way. In time you can make the forgiveness meditation a regular part of your life, letting go of the past and opening your heart to each new moment with a wise, loving kindness.

Creative Approach

Creative activities—and the creative approach to life that often accompanies them—can help us better withstand the huffing and puffing of UnBalancer.

Creative activities are rewarding outlets for self-expression. They give us a sense of accomplishment, often have a centering effect, and they're usually fun to do. But besides these obvious benefits, creative activities can also enhance how we approach our lives.

When we work creatively, we dive deep into ourselves. We pause, look at what we are making, check inside and ask, "Is this working?" and then bring up something of value that we might otherwise never have discovered.

Each time we do this pause/look/check/incorporate cycle, we further nourish our capacity for diving deep. Because our brains get better at doing whatever they do, the more we practice diving deep, the better we get at it—not only with creative activities, but also more generally.

Regularly doing creative activities can facilitate the development of a broader tendency to dive deep, allowing us to become increasingly proficient at sensing and more fully responding to ourselves and the world around us. This increased capacity for sensing and responding helps us more effectively deal with change.

When we are able only to access our superficial thoughts and feelings, our responses to changing circumstances are likely to be limited in their effectiveness. It's as if we are trying to move an iceberg by pushing on its tip, the part we can see. We may manage to lean it over, but it will soon spring back. But when we dive deep and experience the world as our full selves, we can forge ahead more surely.

Diving deep allows us to travel below the water's surface in our mental/emotional submarine, where we can take in the whole

iceberg, home in on its center of gravity, and exert our efforts exactly there. The movement that results may be smaller, but what moves stays moved.

I often see this dive-deep/move-forward-surely process in my work with therapy clients. Those who make the most profound changes may begin a session by simply describing what's going on. But then they pause, check in with some murkier, less clear part of themselves, and bring to the surface something they would otherwise have missed.

For instance, they may begin by describing a situation that made them angry. "When he did that," they might say, "I was so mad…" And then they pause. "Well, it wasn't just that I was mad. I got mad, yes… but really, I was hurt."

They arrive at a more complete understanding, and then deal not only with the surface feeling of anger, but also with the hurt that triggered it.

Diving deep through creative work can encourage positive life changes.

Engaging in a creative activity can not only train the brain to dive deeper, it can also lead to changes in what we do with our lives. People often make meaningful, long-lasting life changes when they engage in creative projects.

I've been engaged with both long-term and short-term creative projects most of my adult life, but I didn't think much about their psychological benefits until I had a near-death experience while a PhD student in English in the early 1990s. I struggled with its meaning and was prompted by a professor to write about it.

Through the process of creating a story, I was able to examine the experience differently than I did in my day-to-day life, in therapy, or in a support group I attended. One of the most profound outcomes was that I abandoned my English PhD and returned to grad school to become a psychotherapist.

Even when people don't make dramatic career or other lifestyle changes, working on creative projects has widespread positive effects. Here's how some of the people I've known have described the benefits of creative work:

Calming. "Writing fiction has a great calming effect. I forget time and hunger and fatigue and enter another, rejuvenating world."

Meditative. "There's a meditative aspect to having a creative practice, in my case painting. It allows me to be in the moment. It's complex, but in a way that energizes. If I'm painting, I'm sane. If I'm not painting, I'm insane."

Touchstone. "I like the touchstone effect. When I'm not doing something creative, it's too easy to get caught up in the demands and responsibilities of my day job and how exhausting that can be."

Nourishing. "I find creative projects a source of nourishment. To see that portion of the journey and think, 'Oh, wow, that's great! I really did that? That came out really well.' Or to go back to another part and think, 'I really struggled with that.' Going back to it keeps on giving back."

Spiritual. "When you start a project, there's a lot of planning, and the goal is far away. It can be a spiritual journey, going from point A to point B."

Evolving. "It's a process of becoming. The artwork evolves, but you evolve, too."

Transformative. "The nature of making art—good art—requires going deeply within and getting in touch with your deepest feelings. This can be difficult—you might revisit past trauma or unpleasant situations. But it can also connect you with exalting joy and even bring on an extreme or altered state of consciousness."

Sustaining. "If you have a project you're working on, you're not alone and you don't feel lonely. I think there's great solace in that. It's a very deep relationship—like the relationship some people have with God."

What to do:

1. **If you're already doing something creative, keep doing it!** If you've stopped, start again. Creative work can be calming, meditative, nourishing, even transformative, in ways that may not be obvious right away, but that become evident over time.

2. **If you don't do anything that feels creative, experiment with different art forms and activities**. Begin with the forms of creativity you enjoy taking in. If you like to read, consider

writing. If you like to listen to music, consider learning to play an instrument and/or composing. If you like to look at art, consider painting, photography, sculpture, pottery. If you like movies, consider acting—or making movies yourself. If none of these "takes," then experiment with other ways to be creative. Creativity is not limited to traditional forms of art. For instance, if you enjoy walking in gardens, consider starting one.

3. **Dive deep.** To train your brain to respond more fully to yourself and your surroundings, do something creative on a regular basis, then practice applying the dive-deep/move-forward-surely process of creative work to your daily life.

Experimental Attitude

As discussed in more depth in Chapter 6, "The Experiment," maintaining an experimental attitude toward life keeps us more open to experiences and to other people and helps us be more resilient in the face of difficulties.

When we have an experimental attitude, we can face our lives with open minds, guided by curiosity. Instead of conforming to the limits of past patterns, we can try things out, see what happens, and adjust our view of reality—and our next steps—accordingly. When things shift in unanticipated ways, we can say, "That *was* my path, but *this* is my path now," adapting to the present moment as it arrives.

An experimental attitude gives our ReBalancers the power to craft new strategies on the fly whenever new challenges occur. These strategies are always there whenever we need them, helping us deal effectively with whatever life (and UnBalancer) hands us.

Putting it All Together

In this chapter, we've taken a look at some of the best ways I've found to make Balancer a better Balancer and you a more balanced you.

Begin to incorporate them into your life. Delve into the strategies, activities, and practices that feel most attractive to you now and let yourself experience them. Explore, experiment, and have fun with each new technique and practice, and let curiosity and an experimental attitude guide you to the next one.

Take your time. There's no hurry.

13. Mix in Mindfulness

He will win who, prepared himself, waits to take the enemy unprepared.

- **Sun Tzu**, *The Art of War*

At the risk of stating the obvious, in order for Balancer to keep us balanced, it's helpful to do activities that explicitly promote ... balance!

Mindfulness-based activities are at the top of the list.

The term **mindfulness**—the state of being focused on the present moment, without judgement—has become part of the zeitgeist in the past several years, and for good reason. Practicing mindfulness promotes positive changes in the body and the brain.

Increasing mindfulness can:

- **Relax muscles** and decrease blood pressure.

- **Reduce stress**, anxiety, unproductive rumination, and emotional reactivity.

- **Promote empathy** and self-compassion.

- **Improve working memory**, focus, self-insight, and intuition.

Over time, practicing mindfulness also reminds us that we don't have to stay on every mental train we find ourselves on. When we notice we've been kidnapped by a thought, worry, emotion, physical sensation, or distraction, we can get off that train and return to the station.

Three basic ways to develop mindfulness include:

1. **Mindfulness-based activities.** Imported from Eastern cultures, practices specifically developed to increase mindfulness include sitting and walking meditation, yoga, tai chi, and chi-gong.

2. **Recreational activities with a mindfulness intention.** When practiced with a mindful, in-the-moment intention, activities such as running, working out, gardening, bicycling, and even motorcycling can promote mindfulness.

3. **Approaching mundane tasks with a mindfulness intention.** Household chores such as washing the dishes, vacuuming, or folding laundry become a form of meditation when we allow ourselves to pay attention to the process of the task itself, rather than hurrying through it to get to the next thing.

Meditation

Meditation is the easiest mindfulness activity to describe fully in writing, but much of this chapter also applies to other Eastern-based mindfulness practices.

Many people think meditation is complicated or difficult, but it isn't. It's literally as simple as breathing, and a good place to begin meditating is with a three-breath meditation repeated throughout the day.

At a retreat I attended years ago, I was introduced to the three-breath meditation through the tolling of the **Mindfulness Bell.**

At random times throughout each day, when someone sounded a bell, we all had to stop what we were doing and take three slow, abdominal breaths.

Whenever the bell rang during the retreat, we halted in mid-sentence, mid-stride, mid-chew, as if we were in a big game of freeze tag. At first this interruption annoyed me. I was in the midst of spiritual evolution, damn it! But by the time the retreat ended, I'd embraced these "interruptions."

When you take an abdominal breath, your belly goes out when you inhale and in when you exhale, the opposite of how many of us breathe. The result is slower, deeper, more concentrated, more efficient respiration. The popular term for it is **belly breathing**.

If you're unfamiliar with belly breathing, you can practice by lying down on a bed or couch and putting one hand on your belly. Close your eyes and breathe naturally. Notice how your belly rises with each intake of breath and falls as you breathe out. This is the way babies breathe.

At the retreat, each time the bell sounded, I was able to stop what I was doing, saying, or thinking. Then I could do a reset. With each slow breath, I asked myself, Do I need to be thinking or feeling what I'm thinking and feeling? Do I want to do what I am about to do? Learning to be still in the midst of life, even briefly, helped me reevaluate these choices.

I have often recommended this three-breath meditation to clients, suggesting that they use any interrupting sound, such as a car horn or a phone's ringing, as a substitute for the Mindfulness Bell.

The effects of this simple change can be revolutionary.

One client whose life was ruled by chaos found this practice to be more valuable than anything else we'd done in therapy. At a street corner on the way to work, hearing the Mindfulness Bell of a car horn, she could think, "I don't really want to waste my time partying tonight." About to leave for a bar, pausing on the first ring of her cell phone, she could see how the evening would play out and decide, "Not this time." Hearing a siren blare in the midst of pangs of guilt or shame, she could choose to forgive herself.

An anxious client found a Mindfulness Bell app for his smartphone and programmed it to sound a gong randomly throughout the day. He was often on the road for his job, and while driving, his mind inevitably went to worrying. When the gong sounded, he took three breaths and allowed himself to return to a more centered place. Over time, not only did his anxiety lessen, but he started to tune in to his true desires and made major positive changes in his career and relationships.

I also continue this practice. When I step into my office and turn on my computer, I hear its Mindfulness Bell beep, reminding me to pause for a moment and assume my best self. Brief meditations throughout the day help me shift gears between clients, return to center, and reinhabit that best self again and again.

Once you get the hang of the three-breath meditation, consider adding other forms of meditation to your day.

Sitting meditation is usually done with eyes closed, seated on a cushion or chair, in a quiet space. The breath-oriented meditation is a simple, time-honored approach. Focus on the intake and exhalation of each breath, imagining the air entering your body, expanding your lungs, and then leaving it as you exhale. If your attention drifts to something else, gently bring it back to your breath. Sitting in the morning for 10-20 minutes helps to start the day in a more centered way, but if the mornings won't work for you, meditating any time of the day is okay.

Walking meditation is another way to reinforce mindfulness. Traditionally, it's practiced by walking slowly back and forth or in a circle while focusing on the breath, the feeling of your feet touching and lifting from the ground, and the physical sensations you take in from your surroundings. However, if you have a regular walk you take recreationally, or even a short walk from the parking lot to your job, you can take these walks in the same mindful manner, with the same centering result.

Mindful recreation. Applying mindful attention to an activity like swimming or running is another way to generate the restorative and balance-enhancing effects of movement-based meditation. I recommend starting first with mindful walking, and then, when you feel comfortable with the cycle of losing attention and restoring it, experiment with translating this mindful approach to your chosen activity.

Mindful attitude. One of my favorite ways to incorporate mindfulness into life is to perform daily tasks with a mindful attitude. Taking a shower, brushing your teeth, and eating, if done without distraction and with a focus on your physical actions, can become a regular mindfulness practice.

Even chores, done mindfully, can become centering meditations. For example, the **"washing the dishes"** meditation is often suggested by meditation teachers and is one I do myself.

As a child, my brother Mike and I did most of the household chores, including washing dishes and putting them away, and as a result I've never much liked that task. So I've turned it into a meditation.

I let the dishes pile up during the day and then wash them deliberately at night. I pay attention to the sound of the running water, the feel of the soap and sponge, the transformation of each dish from dirty to clean. The dishwashing takes the same few minutes it would if I were listening to music, thinking about what else I wanted to do that evening, or just pushing through an unpleasant chore. But instead of feeling slightly agitated during or afterward, as I once did, I now feel relaxed and refreshed.

Not long ago, I discovered that this specific meditation had potential side benefits.

I was working with an anxious 12-year-old boy, the oldest of several siblings. His parents wanted me to teach him to meditate. So we tried sitting meditation, but he couldn't sit still. We tried walking meditation, but he found it boring. Then I thought of dishwashing meditation. I gathered up the few cups and dishes in my office and put them in the sink, and I had him toss in a few of the washable toys. "Now," I said, "squirt some dish soap on the sponge, and I'll show you how to do dishwashing meditation."

I explained the process and for about five minutes he carefully and attentively washed the dishes and the toys. As he dried the last dish, he turned to me and said he felt much calmer. Then he added, gleefully, "And my mother will love this! I have a big family, and we have a lot of dirty dishes!"

Try turning any regular chore you don't much care for into a meditation and you may experience the same mini-transformation—and perhaps also the same glee!

What to do:

1. **Mindfulness practices.** Try an Eastern-based practice designed to enhance mindfulness such as sitting or walking meditation, yoga, tai chi, or chi-gong. These practices have been demonstrated to reduce stress and anxiety, improve focus, relax the body, and increase resilience. Consider starting with a simple three-breath meditation, as described earlier in this chapter.

2. **Mindful recreation.** If you are already a runner, swimmer, walker, bicyclist, or you participate in another recreational activity, approaching what you already do with a mindfulness attitude will generate many of the same beneficial effects as a mindfulness practice such as walking meditation. Pay attention to each moment and, if you find yourself drifting, bring your attention back to the present. Then rinse, lather, and repeat (as they used to say on shampoo bottles).

3. **Mindful chores.** Instead of just powering through daily tasks and chores, practice mindful dishwashing, vacuuming, laundry folding, tooth brushing, and notice the subtle benefits, both in the moment and over time.

14. Uncertainty, Allies, and Confederates

Danger has a bracing effect.
- **Sun Tzu**, *The Art of War*

The Monk, the Tigers, and the Strawberry

There once was a Zen monk who, while walking across a field, encountered a ferocious tiger. The tiger chased the monk across the field until he reached the edge of a high cliff. The monk's only chance was to grab a vine that grew at the cliff's edge and lower himself out of the tiger's reach. As the monk hung from the vine, he saw that below him, another tiger was waiting. He also noticed two mice starting to gnaw on the vine.

What could the monk do now?

Uncertainty

Although few of us are literally pursued by tigers above and below, most of us have to deal with one of UnBalancer's chief confederates, **Uncertainty**. And if we haven't yet, we will soon enough.

Confederate is the term I'm using for UnBalancer's many accomplices. These include unbalancers such as Illness, Accident, Loss, Misfortune, Entropy, Chance, Obliviousness, Fear, Greed, Distrust, Anger, Hatred, Doubt, Jealousy, and any of the myriad external and internal forces that can knock us out of alignment.

For many of us, the most potent confederate is Uncertainty.

We're uncertain about what will happen in our relationships, the economy, the climate; how people see us; how an undertaking will go; how our children will do in school, and in life; what will become of us as we age. And no matter who we are and what we have accomplished, we are uncertain about our own end—when it will occur, what will cause it, whether we will suffer, how we will be remembered, what will happen afterward.

The only thing we can *really* be certain of is Uncertainty.

With more acute unbalancers, there's a sudden blow to our internal gyroscopes that makes us tilt, then after a recovery process we move on. Uncertainty isn't like that. Instead, it can feel like a constant pressure, pushing us steadily down—one that, if it goes on long enough, with enough force, grinds our bearings into grit.

Some years ago, I moved a couple of thousand books and vinyl records from Buffalo to Boston, filling not only the trunk but also the front and back seats of my car with heavy boxes. By the time I got close to home, I could hear a low whine from the left rear wheel well, close to where the heaviest boxes, containing my record collection, sat. Within days, the car began to rumble. Then it screamed. The constant weight had worn out that wheel bearing.

Uncertainty can be like that.

Many of us try to combat Uncertainty by creating an illusion of certainty. We anticipate a worst-case or best-case scenario. It comforts us to pretend our projection is real, but it's only a shadow on a wall.

When we cling to the best case, we may become complacent and fail to strive for the best outcome. When we dread the worst case, we may grow hypervigilant, seeing only signs of catastrophe. Our projections enable us to sidestep Uncertainty, but often at a terrible cost in ignorance and anxiety.

Others follow the adage, "Hope for the best but expect the worst." We keep up a positive attitude, but we also steel ourselves for disaster. We keep our spare tires inflated, save for a rainy day, buy bread and bottled water when the forecast calls for a storm, and hope to keep Uncertainty at bay.

Some of us go one better and create multiple backup plans. Like good Boy Scouts, our motto is "Be Prepared."

My father, a Boy Scout leader for many years, lived by this credo. He had duplicates, and in some cases triplicates, of all the vital parts of the devices in our house … just in case. Stacked beside his workbench were two or three replacement motors for the washing machine and the dryer. Shelves in a nearby closet overflowed with duplicate faucets, belts, hoses, clamps, fasteners, and other spare parts. We could have stocked a small hardware store with all that stuff. Yet none of these backups were a bulwark against his failing heart.

These are typical Balancer strategies for getting us through the anxiety of Uncertainty, and sometimes they're effective. But often, optimism, hypervigilance, platitudes, and even backup plans aren't enough.

That's when the gleam appears in UnBalancer's eyes.

Balancer Allies

Fortunately, just as UnBalancer has its Confederates, so Balancer has its **Allies**.

When Balancer starts to tilt, its first line of defense is ReBalancer, its Chief of Staff. Often, ReBalancer, drawing on its storehouse of tools, techniques, and strategies, as well as its experimental attitude, is equal to the task. But in the face of a powerful combatant like Uncertainty, we may also need to call in other members of Balancer's cadre.

Balancer's Allies include Acceptance, Logic, Intuition, Common Sense, Courage, Gratitude, Moderation, Patience, Perseverance, Support, and the many other internal and external resources that can help restore equilibrium.

These are all powerful Allies. When even ReBalancer has run out of steam, they can throw in a hand and save the day.

Allies and Confederates sometimes square off directly. Acceptance is the antidote to loss, courage to fear, hope to despair. Similarly, perseverance will overcome procrastination, developing patience will tame impulsiveness, and support relieves isolation.

But when the tigers are above and the tigers are below, and the mice are gnawing on your vine, you need to pull out all the stops and call in Balancer's ultimate Ally.

That Ally is **Presence**.

Presence vs. Uncertainty

Let's return to the monk hanging from his cliff:

As the vine began to give way, with death imminent, the monk also saw a ripe wild strawberry growing on the cliff wall. Clutching the vine with one hand, he plucked the strawberry with the other.

He put it in his mouth.

"This lovely strawberry," he thought. "How sweet it tastes."

Those who deal most effectively with potentially paralyzing Uncertainty respond very differently from those who succumb to it.

Instead of catastrophizing, exhausting their energy on worry and backup plans, or escaping from their fears with alcohol, drugs, or distraction, they turn their focus to the present. They remain alert to whatever they must do to try to ensure a desired outcome, but they are also fully engaged in everything else in their lives.

Instead of putting everything else on hold when faced with uncertain health, an uncertain relationship, or an uncertain political or economic time, those who vanquish Uncertainty savor the life they have, in each moment. They know that whatever they are uncertain of will, in time, become a certainty, but they are in no hurry to get there.

They are fully present, and Uncertainty has no power over Presence.

They eat the wild strawberry growing on the cliff wall.

The Diving Bell and the Butterfly

There are everyday examples of this practice, and there are dramatic ones. One particularly striking example comes to mind: the case of Jean-Dominique Bauby.

Bauby, a Parisian journalist and magazine editor, was stricken, at age 43, with a massive stroke that put him into a coma for 20 days. When he awoke, he was completely aware and alert but also nearly paralyzed, able only to swivel his head slightly and to blink his left eye. His mind was locked in his body and he had almost no way to communicate his thoughts, feelings, and needs to the outside world.

Miraculously, we know what happened to him because he wrote a book about his experiences, *The Diving Bell and the Butterfly: A Memoir of Life in Death*, from inside this locked-in state.

He wrote his book literally one letter at a time, blinking his left eye while a transcriber recited the French alphabet in order of letter frequency, recording a character when Bauby blinked to indicate his choice. Each word took about two minutes to write and the entire book took 200,000 blinks.

It's been almost 20 years since I read Bauby's book, but the contrast between his external and internal worlds is still vivid.

Although he remained completely aware of his condition and surroundings, Bauby found a way to have a full and meaningful life in what most of us would consider unendurable conditions. He lived mainly in his imagination.

Take, for example, his experience of food. Bauby had been something of a food connoisseur and he'd enjoyed many fine meals. After his stroke, he was fed through tubes, perhaps never to eat again. Facing this tiger above and tiger below, he "ate" like a king by recalling past meals and rearranging them in his mind.

He traveled widely—in his mind. "My diving bell becomes less oppressive," he wrote, "and my mind takes flight like a butterfly. There is so much to do. You can wander off in space or in time, set out for Tierra del Fuego or for King Midas's court. You can visit the woman you love, slide down beside her and stroke her still-sleeping face. You can build castles in Spain, steal the Golden Fleece, discover Atlantis, realize your childhood dreams and adult ambitions."

Like the Zen monk in our story, he found the strawberry and savored it, dealing with the terror and Uncertainty of his fate by seizing each moment.

Bauby died from pneumonia two days after his book was published. *The Diving Bell and the Butterfly* sold 25,000 copies on the first day it was available, became the number one bestseller in Europe, and was later made into a well-received film.

Often, we think we are on one path only to find, somewhere down the line, that we have actually been on another without knowing it. We are rattled, and until we become present to the life we are in *now*, we can dwell in a branch of purgatory managed by Uncertainty. But once we see that this path is, simply, another path, we are free to take in everything that we find along its way. We hold onto the vine and reach for the strawberry and see how sweet it tastes.

15. Stay Sane with the Personal Craziness Index

To win one hundred victories in one hundred battles is not the acme of skill. To subdue the enemy without fighting is the acme of skill.

- **Sun Tzu**, *The Art of War*

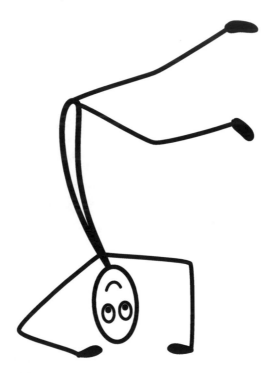

To stay sane in an insane world, we need more than new tools and techniques. To maintain sanity, we also have to *keep doing the things that got us there.*

The final piece of the resilience puzzle is to build Balancer-enhancing attitudes and practices into our daily lives, so they are as much a part of our routines as breathing. Then we keep watch to make sure we're staying on track.

When Balancer incorporates the new tools ReBalancer used to get us back in gear, it gets stronger. Self-care becomes something we do every day, not just when stress is high. The Experiment becomes an experimental attitude we carry with us 24/7.

Balancer fitness conditioners also build resilience. To enhance our readiness for whatever UnBalancer sends our way, we incorporate them into our routines. We adopt meditation as a daily practice. Self-compassion and radical acceptance become the new norm. We practice presence whenever we can. And so on.

But maintaining new habits takes persistence, and if we don't stay on top of our game, we run the risk of drifting back to our old, less resilient ways.

UnBalancer loves when that happens!

So we need a method for regularly checking in with ourselves to make sure we're continuing to use all the shiny new tools and techniques we worked so hard to acquire.

The PCI

To help stay on track, I recommend using a monitoring tool called the **Personal Craziness Index (PCI).**

The PCI was first presented by author and psychologist Patrick J. Carnes in his groundbreaking book on addiction recovery, *A Gentle Path through the Twelve Steps: The Classic Guide for All People in the Process of Recovery*. But it turns out that the PCI has uses beyond maintaining sobriety, and one of them is to monitor resilience.

The PCI is a universal tracking tool that can be used by anyone to monitor and maintain balance. It relies on the fact that, in both subtle and obvious ways, we respond to aspects of our lives differently when we're in balance and when we're not.

The PCI is a build-it-yourself tool. In each of 10 major life areas, the PCI lists three indicators of how we act when we are in balance. Then we track the seven most significant ones every day.

The best ones to track are those you can easily see you are doing or not doing. Below, you can see an example of a completed PCI, with the tracked activities in **bold** and marked with an asterisk (*).

HEALTH/HYGIENE	RECREATION
1. Go to gym 3x/week	1. Plan/take 2 vacation trips/year
2. Cook own meals *	2. Go to movies with gf or friends
3. Sleep at least seven hours/night	**3. Take daily walk in morning ***
HOUSING	FAMILY
1. Make bed in the morning	1. Call/email family regularly
2. Wash dishes after each meal *	2. Send birthday cards
3. Keep clutter to a minimum	3. Visit family at least once/month
TRANSPORTATION	FRIENDS
1. Fill tank when it reaches ¼ full	1. Call or email friends regularly
2. Keep up with car maintenance	2. Meet friends at least once/week
3. Keep inside of car clean	3. Send birthday cards
WORK/MONEY	GROUP ACTIVITIES
1. Pay bills when I get them *	1. Attend creativity group regularly
2. Maintain bank account buffer	2. Contribute to online groups
3. Limit work to 40hrs/week *	3. Go to weekly poker game
HOBBIES/INTERESTS	SPIRITUALITY
1. Work on photos once/week	**1. Meditate daily ***
2. Read every night *	2. Go to Buddhist group regularly
3. Write at least 3x/week	3. Listen to spiritual podcasts

When I first heard about the PCI, I used it with addict clients as a relapse-prevention tool. But then I wondered how it would work with other problems.

So, like Dr. Marshall and his ulcer study (see Chapter 6, "The Experiment"), I conducted an Experiment on myself. Would this tool also work for the low-level depression I often experienced when I was overworked, or when winter's darkness set in?

My own PCI was much like the example above. My Experiment turned out to be successful in keeping depression at bay, even in the depths of winter.

Since then, I've used the PCI with many clients with a wide variety of issues that unbalance them. For those who not only complete the PCI but also track it daily, it has become an essential tool in maintaining their personal sanity.

Tracking

Without tracking, the PCI is of limited use. With it, it's as valuable as a GPS for staying the course.

When we start to slip into unbalanced behaviors, chances are we're headed for a major tilt in the near future unless we take corrective actions. What's nice about PCI tracking is that, in addition to alerting us that corrective actions are needed, the course corrections themselves are built into the tool.

Most of the time, all we have to do to restore balance is resume any Balancer activities we've stopped doing, and stop any unbalancing activities that snuck back in.

To select the most significant PCI items to track, think about which behaviors are most clearly different when you're in balance and when you're not. Then track those items every day.

Here's what a few days of PCI tracking looks like for the sample PCI:

Cooking	1		1					1	1						
Dishes	1		1				1	1	1						
Bills	1	1	1	1	1	1		1	1						
Reading	1	1			1	1	1	1	1						
Work	1	1	1			1	1	1							
Walks	1		1	1	1	1	1	1							
Meditation	1	1	1		1	1	1	1	1						
PCI	7	4	6	2	4	5	5	7	6						
	9/1	9/2	9/3	9/4	9/5	9/6	9/7	9/8	9/9	9/10	9/11	9/12	9/13	9/14	9/15

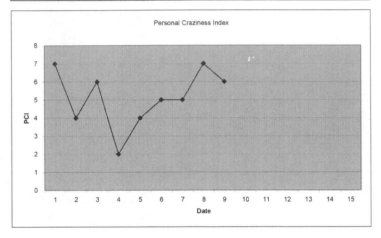

Personal Craziness Index

NOTE: You can download an editable PCI template and a tracking spreadsheet from the Transformations Press resources page: transformationspress.org/resources/nonfiction-resources

For instance, suppose that in the "Health/Hygiene" category, we wrote that when we're feeling balanced, we go to the gym three times a week, cook our own meals, and sleep at least seven hours per night. Although each of these actions alone may seem unimportant, as indicators that Balancer is humming along smoothly they are invaluable.

Now let's say that for you, cooking your own meals is the clearest indicator in the "Health/Hygiene" category—you almost always cook when you're doing well, and you almost always pick up takeout or eat out when you're not. That's an indicator you'll want to track.

In the other categories, let's say (as in this example) we've identified washing dishes, paying bills on time, limiting work to 40 hours per week, reading every night, morning walks, and daily meditation as things we do when we're balanced and things we tend not to do when we're not.

If we notice we're picking up junk food, or letting dishes pile up in the sink, or waiting till the last minute to pay bills, or skipping our reading, walks, or meditation, our PCI lets us know that we're also more vulnerable to imminent imbalance.

Detecting mild imbalance before UnBalancer gathers enough strength to pull us under is much easier than restoring balance after we've been toppled.

If we're off on only one or two indicators, we've given up only a little ground, and out-maneuvering UnBalancer is easy: We *will* ourselves to go back to cooking. We wash the dishes. We pay bills on time, or resume the reading, walks, or meditation—or whatever we've been tracking on our individual PCI. As we resume doing these things, our PCI rises and the downward slide reverses.

In 12-step recovery programs, the phrase "fake it till you make it" expresses the idea of using our will to assume new, more self-actualizing attitudes and behaviors. The PCI helps us "fake it till we make it" when the amount of willpower that's required to keep personal craziness at bay is still small. Then we can go forward, Balancer unhindered, UnBalancer thwarted once again.

Using the PCI

Let's revisit burnout as an application of how the PCI can help Balancer prevent disaster.

As you may recall from Chapter 3, "ReBalancer to the Rescue," the winter of 2014/2015 broke Boston's all-time seasonal snowfall record, unbalanced many of my former clients, and, ultimately, unbalanced me, too.

Every week for 14 weeks, former clients contacted me about getting back into therapy. That winter and spring, I accepted them all, overwhelming my schedule and my personal balance. The result: burnout.

UnBalancer won that round, and it took me a long time to recover.

But let's look ahead and imagine another terrible winter occurs a couple of years down the road. Only this time, I'm using the PCI.

1. After the first few clients start returning, I notice that I'm having to squeeze more clients in my day than I know, from experience, are healthy for me to handle. This has become one of my new PCI tracking items.

2. Because I'm also tracking self-care, I notice that I'm starting to put off doing it.

3. Instead of calling in ReBalancer to rescue me from another UnBalancer victory, Balancer itself detects the early warning signs of imbalance.

4. Recognizing that my PCI has started to drop, I realize I have to stop, evaluate what's going on, and make some course corrections.

5. Before my PCI gets so low that I'm in dangerous territory, I start taking mini-breaks instead of filling all available time with clients, and I add other restorative activities, making sure I get the sleep I need to handle the additional stress of my distressed clients.

6. And I feel okay about saying "Sorry, I can't see you right now." I tell my potential returning clients that I can see them only after my schedule frees up. Some of them agree to ap-

pointments several weeks ahead. Others ask me for referrals to other therapists, which I accommodate.

7. I resume my full self-care activities.

8. Burnout is prevented, balance restored, and Balancer is still in charge.

Instead of the sleep-deprived, overcaffeinated, exhausted therapist I could have become, I'm able to maintain my previous level of balance despite the efforts of UnBalancer to unhinge me. Yes, some clients have to wait a few weeks and others find other therapists, but overall, everyone gets the care they need—including me!

What to do:

1. **Create Your Personal Craziness Index.** Use the PCI to track the things you do that keep you sane. The downloadable template provided below has 10 suggested categories for the Personal Craziness Index. If some of these categories don't fit your situation, substitute others that do.

    Under each category, write three indicators that you are in a good place. List the things you do that keep you in positive territory, or things you don't do that also demonstrate that you're functioning well. For example, under "Health/ Hygiene," you might list "exercise 3x per week" as something you do to stay fit, or "don't eat junk food" as a reminder to avoid unhealthy eating.

    NOTE: You can download an editable PCI template and a tracking spreadsheet from the Transformations Press resources page:
    transformationspress.org/resources/nonfiction-resources

2. **Track seven indicators**. Choose the seven indicators, from any of these 10 categories, that most clearly show you're maintaining your defenses against personal craziness.

   At the end of each day, tally up how you did. Give yourself a score from 0 to 7, where "7" is "I'm doing all the positive things / not doing any of the negative things" and "0" is "I'm not doing any of the positive things / doing all of the negative things." Keep a daily log.

   NOTE: You get a "0" for days you don't bother to check!

3. **If your score dips below seven, reverse the trend**. If your numbers start dropping, reverse the trend by resuming the positives on your PCI and avoiding the negatives. When your Personal Craziness Index is restored, your personal craziness will likewise diminish, restoring your personal sanity—and your balance.

4. **IMPORTANT: As conditions change, re-do the PCI** to make sure it clearly tracks the most significant differences between when you are in balance and when UnBalancer is having its way with you.

WRAP-UP:
BALANCE LOST, REGAINED,
MAINTAINED

Victory in war is not repetitious, but adapts its form endlessly. Do not repeat the tactics which have gained you one victory, but let your methods be regulated by the infinite variety of circumstances.

- **Sun Tzu**, *The Art of War*

The Hero's Journey

The Battle for Balance is an epic struggle in the age-old tradition of the Hero's Journey. It is, as we have seen, literally a fight for life, liberty, and the pursuit of happiness.

Hero's Journey stories, whether they are mythological epics like the *Odyssey* or contemporary ones like *Star Wars*, all have a similar structure. It's a structure that Joseph Campbell, author of *The Hero with a Thousand Faces*, found in myths and folktales from around the world, and it's built into human experience.

The arc of Hero's Journey is for the not-quite-hero, through a series of potentially deadly adventures, to rise to the level of hero, returning to his or her world a changed person and bearing an important boon to society.

Hero's Journey stories begin with the would-be heroes living what seem to be okay lives, but beneath the surface they have a character flaw. Soon after the story begins, they are thrust into situations where this hidden flaw is revealed.

The heroes face challenges that turn their worlds upside-down.

The rules they've lived by no longer apply. Encountering one obstacle after another, attacked by enemies in every corner, they suffer defeat after defeat until, finally, they hit bottom.

This is the decisive moment. There they will remain, failed heroes, unless they find their purpose and muster the courage to rise up.

The return trip to the world they knew is as fraught with peril as was the way down, but now they see what they're fighting for, and each challenge makes them more determined. At last they arrive home, mission accomplished, wiser and stronger, and with something to offer their fellow citizens that they could not have provided before their adventures began.

Our Personal Hero's Journeys

The story of losing, regaining, and maintaining balance is a Hero's Journey each of us will experience many times throughout our lives.

All Hero's Journey stories begin in the middle, and so do ours. We have, let's say, been doing fairly well, but something unbalances us to the point where we tilt. Maybe it's a sudden, overwhelming event. Maybe it's a gradual accretion of stresses that brings us to the breaking point—or beyond. Or it could be Uncertainty itself.

Regardless, we have embarked on an adventure, the start of a life-or-death struggle with UnBalancer.

We, too, are thrust into a world where the stability we have known is ripped from under our feet. We, too, suffer a series of defeats until we, too, finally hit bottom. And we, too, may have a hidden weakness that is only revealed—and ultimately overcome—by our journey back to balance.

In all Hero's Journey stories, the heroes face enemies who threaten to destroy them. We, too, face deadly enemies: UnBalancer and his cadre of balance-destroying forces.

In all Hero's Journey stories, the heroes also have friends and fellow travelers without whom they could not prevail. We have Balancer, ReBalancer, and Balancer's many allies.

On all Hero's Journeys, the heroes learn the necessary truths that, without the journey, they might never have learned. We, too, learn from our battles with UnBalancer, and each time we overcome its destructive forces we grow wiser.

On all Hero's Journeys, the heroes return with something of great value to themselves and to their societies. We, too, return with something of great value: By rising from defeat and building our resilience, we realize our full potential as human beings. And from this more elevated vantage point, we can fully engage in the lives around us, paying forward what we have gained from our struggles.

The Balance Monomyth

In *The Hero with a Thousand Faces*, Joseph Cambell outlines the specific stages that define most Hero's Journey stories. He calls this structure the **monomyth**.

The stages of recovery from UnBalancer's actions also have a series of stages we'll call the Balance Monomyth. These are the stages we all go through when we move from victim to victor in our battles with UnBalancer.

The Balance Monomyth consists of six stages: Detect, Assess, Plan, Restore, Integrate, and Monitor/Maintain.

These six stages apply to chronic imbalance situations—the ones that take us down one notch at a time, such as a too-demanding job, a relationship gone awry, or an addictive behavior. And they also apply to acute situations—those that quickly knock us flat, such as a major health crisis, romantic breakup, sudden loss of a job, or the death of someone close.

Here's the basic outline of the Balance Monomyth:

1. **Detect.** Balancer notices when we're starting to tip—or have already gone down for the count.

2. **Assess.** To minimize further damage, Balancer stops what we're doing and calls on ReBalancer to assess the situation.

3. **Plan.** ReBalancer develops a plan to get us back on our feet.

4. **Restore.** ReBalancer executes the plan, patching up our cuts, icing our bruises, wrapping our injured hands, and making sure we can see straight before we return to the fray.

5. **Integrate.** ReBalancer teaches Balancer what it's gleaned from the struggle, better preparing us for UnBalancer's mean left hook and tricky footwork.

6. **Monitor/Maintain.** Moving forward, Balancer keeps a closer watch on UnBalancer, and also maintains new-and-improved strategies to better equip us to emerge victorious in our next encounter with UnBalancer.

Let's see how the Balance Monomyth plays out in both chronic and acute UnBalancer attacks.

Example: Work/Life Imbalance

Chronic stress wears us down little by little.

Some examples: burnout, relationship troubles, career or job issues, financial strife, addiction, the cumulative effects of multiple forms of stress, even a very tough winter. They creep up on us like nocturnal predators, and by the time we notice them, we've already had the rug pulled out from under us.

One of the frequent uses I hear of the word "balance" is about maintaining a healthy work/life balance.

The great American fiction writer William Faulkner, author of *The Sound and the Fury*, once said, "You can't eat for eight hours a day nor drink for eight hours a day nor make love for eight hours a day—all you can do for eight hours is work. Which is the reason why man makes himself and everybody else so miserable and unhappy."

Whether or not you see "work" the way Faulkner did, work sometimes can take up so much time and energy that everything else suffers.

Let's play out how a work/life imbalance can wreak havoc, and how ReBalancer and Balancer can help us restore equilibrium.

1. Detect

Balancer notices when we're starting to tip—or have already gone down for the count.

For example, let's say this is how your work/life balance looks when it's the way you like it:

- You don't work more than eight hours per day or five days a week.

- You take holidays and vacations.

- You have healthy eating habits and sleep well.

- You have time and energy to go to the gym, be with friends and family, and engage in the hobbies and activities that are important to you.

- Your bills are paid on time.

- You're never close to running on empty.

Now let's say that recently, there's been a lot of pressure at your job.

You've started working later or bringing work home, and you've been skimping on the things that keep you even-keeled. You skipped your last vacation, you find yourself eating takeout on the way home, and you're short-changing yourself on sleep and exercise.

Balancer is struggling to stay upright, but for a while you don't see it because the erosion of balance comes on gradually.

You're the frog in the pot, and the water's pretty warm. UnBalancer's licking its lips in gleeful anticipation.

Balancer senses trouble. You move on to Stage 2, Assess.

Or maybe you've already toppled.

You've continued to ignore the early warning symptoms and you're starting to hurt in places you never hurt before. You don't spend time with your kids, your friends, your significant other. You've started drinking, or you stay up half the night lost in video games or Internet porn. The signs of an imminent crash are all too obvious to your friends and family, and even your co-workers are starting to notice.

Balancer's on the ground.

You're the frog in the pot, and the water's boiling. UnBalancer raises a fist in triumph.

You tumble into Stage 2 because there's nowhere left to go.

2. Assess

To minimize further damage, Balancer stops what we're doing and calls on ReBalancer to assess the situation.

Balancer takes a time out.

ReBalancer rolls up its sleeves and gets to work figuring out how you got into this state and what you can take away, modify, or add back into your life to help restore balance.

If you've been tracking your balance with the PCI, you can see that your score has been slipping for a while, and you notice that the slippage coincided with the longer work hours.

You look not only at the seven main activities you've been tracking, but also at all the others, because UnBalancer is tricky, and you may have been tracking the wrong indicators. These untracked areas are also important to maintaining stability, perhaps more important than you realized when you constructed the PCI.

This re-assessment is similar to what the British airforce did during WWII. When planes returned from missions riddled with bullet holes, they looked not only at the damaged parts of each aircraft, but also at the undamaged areas. Those undamaged areas, they reasoned, were the ones that really needed reinforcement because the planes that got hit there didn't make it back.

We're the same way. If you've been using the PCI but UnBalancer got to you anyway, tweak the PCI to more accurately track the early signs of imbalance, and make sure to check it every day.

If you haven't been using the PCI, construct one to help prevent UnBalancer from getting the upper hand again. (See Chapter 15, "Stay Sane with the Personal Craziness Index.")

3. Plan

ReBalancer develops a plan to get us back on our feet.

A major unbalanced state is an emergency and it requires **triage** in order to shorten the time we're down and minimize the damage.

Triage is an approach to problems that's designed to provide the most possible benefit in the shortest time. It's standard procedure in treatment facilities for battlefield casualties. On the battlefield, most of the medics' efforts go to those who are moderately wounded. The lightly wounded might be given cursory treatment, or none at all, and the severely wounded are given morphine to ease the pain of dying.

The same principle can be applied to any task for which there isn't enough time or there aren't enough resources to do the best conceivable job. The part of the job that's most likely to benefit from your efforts is done first, and the parts that are either non-essential, or too time-consuming to do thoroughly, can be done later.

Triage is a ReBalancer strategy. Using tools like the PCI, ReBalancer identifies course corrections, focusing first on the "must haves" before allocating resources to the "nice to haves."

After it's determined the cause of work/life imbalance and assessed the consequences, ReBalancer creates an action plan for restoring equilibrium.

ReBalancer uses tools like the Medicine Wheel to help envision what your body, mind, and spirit need in order to recover. Or the Circles of Problems and Resources, which connect the problems you're experiencing with the resources you need to solve them. Or the Miracle Question, which helps you see the "solved problem" version of your life in detail, and also provides a methodology for getting there, one doable step at a time. (See Chapter 4, "Assess and Plan.")

ReBalancer uses these tools to help you re-imagine your life with a healthy balance between work and everything else, so you feel satisfied on a physical, emotional, psychological, spiritual, relational, and material level.

Then ReBalancer develops a step-by-step plan to get there.

In this work/life imbalance example, ReBalancer determines that returning to a 40-hour work week will yield the most immediate benefits by opening up time to do the self-care, connection, recreational, and spiritual activities that have gone by the wayside.

Then it continues the triage process to help you prioritize the activities that will be the most helpful first. The exact mix will be different for each of us, but self-care practices such as sleeping well and eating healthy foods, and physical activities such as working out at the gym or taking walks, are high on the "Do this first" list, along with reconnecting to friends, family, and other supportive social connections.

During this stage, ReBalancer might conclude that an important course correction for you, either immediately or down the road, is a job or career change. ReBalancer tools can connect you with resources for determining what might be a better job or career, then map out a strategy for transitioning.

4. Restore

ReBalancer executes the plan, patching up our cuts, icing our bruises, wrapping our injured hands, and making sure we can see straight before we return to the fray.

As the work week ratchets back to 40 hours, free time opens up again.

ReBalancer guides you through execution of the plan, step-by-step, restoring what was lost in the vortex of overwork, eliminating stresses where possible, adding in supports and activities, and experimenting with new resilience-enhancing activities.

Mini self-care can re-introduce necessary, nourishing activities even before you've opened up space and time for full-fledged self care. Adopting a personal flywheel activity can increase resilience by providing a steady-state touchstone. And The Experiment can help you find new ways to recover the vibrancy you've lost. (See Chapters 5 and 6, "Restore Balance" and "The Experiment.")

During the Restore stage, you start to resemble a country music song played backwards: You get your time back, you get your health back, you get your relationships back, you get your life back.

The "before" and "after" are dramatic.

Before, you felt chronically stressed and worn out, up in the middle of the night worrying about all the things you hadn't done. Now, you sleep peacefully and wake each day with optimism and energy. Before, you suffered from assorted aches, pains, and illnesses. Now, you're full of energy again. Before, you were grumpy and irritable with your significant others, family, and friends. Now, you're their hero, a model of what's needed to stay in balance.

5. Integrate

ReBalancer teaches Balancer what it's gleaned from the struggle, better preparing us for UnBalancer's mean left hook and fancy footwork.

ReBalancer has one more task.

To stay on top of UnBalancer, Balancer must incorporate what ReBalancer has implemented, or your victory over UnBalancer will be short-lived.

So, you build a firm boundary around not working overtime, taking vacations, keeping weekends open for friends, family, and R&R. You schedule time for the things you've added back into your life and any new balance-enhancing skills and activities you've picked up.

You recognize that self-care is the essential foundation for everything else you do.

6. Monitor/Maintain

Moving forward, Balancer keeps a closer watch on UnBalancer, and also maintains new-and-improved strategies to better equip us to emerge the victor in our next encounter with UnBalancer.

Control goes back to Balancer.

You've recovered from a shock and now you're a happy camper. Balancer is back online, doing what Balancer does. The trick now is to stay on track. You'd rather not go through this again, if you can help it.

Balancer takes a detailed look at where you are now, what you've been through, what helped you recover, and how to prevent a future collapse.

Balancer asks questions like: Were there warning signs you missed completely? Were there some you ignored? Is what happened to you part of a pattern? Where did it come from? What new practices do you now do to stay balanced? Are there other practices that might help enhance your self-awareness, watchfulness, and resilience?

You see clearly how sneaky UnBalancer can be, and you're determined to keep it at bay.

You fine-tune the PCI so you can catch the early warning signs and make course corrections before things get out of hand. You resolve not only to use the PCI regularly, but also to revisit it from time to time, making sure that it's truly tracking the most meaningful indicators.

You've not only returned to balance, you've got a better Balancer.

Example: Major Loss

Chronic stress brings us down a bit at a time, and as we strengthen and educate Balancer, we can get better at spotting it before UnBalancer has his way with us. But UnBalancer has another tactic that's at least as unbalancing, and it's often impossible to prevent.

Acute stress happens when a sudden, overwhelmingly difficult event occurs, such as a romantic breakup, divorce, serious illness, major car accident, identity theft, the death of a loved one, or another loss of similar magnitude.

When acute stress hits, even the most resilient Balancers are usually knocked flat.

But the same stages that help us recover from chronic stress also guide us when acute stress bowls us over. The specific ReBalancer and Balancer actions are different, but the basic algorithm still applies.

Let's look, here, at how these six stages apply after a major breakup or the death of a loved one.

1. Detect

Balancer notices when we're starting to tip—or have already gone down for the count.

There's nothing subtle about detecting when a sudden loss occurs. Regardless of the nature of the relationship, a major breakup or the death of a close relative or friend is immediately unbalancing. It's as if we've been punched in the gut. The wind is knocked out of us and we're laid out flat.

And that's how it should be. Something has radically changed. Becoming unbalanced by grief, confusion, and other difficult emotions is a normal response, and restoring true balance can take substantial time and effort.

However, as with a breakdown from chronic stress, there are actions that help with recovery and there are also actions that can work against it.

Making radical changes quickly, or escaping into addictive behaviors to avoid change, are two responses that can slow recovery.

Let's look at some that help.

2. Assess

To minimize further damage, Balancer stops what we're doing and calls on ReBalancer to assess the situation.

Recovering from a sudden loss is often a longer and less deliberate process than recovery from chronic stress.

We may move through the first stages of recovery with a vague numbness, unable to fully take in what's happened. Or, conversely, we are so shaken that our lives before this loss seem impossible to relate to. Only gradually do we come to fully grasp what has stayed the same, and what is irrevocably altered.

In the assessment stage, the first and most important ReBalancer action is to acknowledge that the parameters of our lives have changed. Who we were before and who we will become won't ever be quite the same. There may be no "normal" to return to, and it may be months, or even years, before we can fully incorporate the loss into our lives and continue on with acceptance and renewed energy.

Initially, recognition of this changed reality will come and go.

Denial is usually the first stage of recovery from a major loss, and moving between feeling that the loss is real and unreal is how we have evolved to adapt to loss. We naturally let in only as much as we can handle.

After the initial shock has been absorbed, ReBalancer can do a more detailed assessment.

ReBalancer focuses on doing the things that need to be done first. Depending on the type of loss, this can involve actions such as finding a divorce mediator or attorney, making funeral arrangements, dividing possessions, and determining what to do with a deceased loved ones' business. None of this is easy, but denial and its close cousin, compartmentalizing, shield us from some of the grief.

3. Plan

ReBalancer develops a plan to get us back on our feet.

After a major breakup or a death, it can feel as if the cable connecting one heart to another's has been ripped out.

The five stages of loss, described by Elizabeth Kubler Ross in her book *On Grief and Grieving* are well known: denial, anger, bargaining, depression, and acceptance. But no two instances of grief are the same. We're all in uncharted territory when a major loss occurs, with only a rough map of the terrain to guide us and no clear sense of how long the journey will take.

ReBalancer recognizes that grieving has its own pace and can't be hurried.

As we move through the first period of mourning, and denial begins to fade, ReBalancer helps us navigate changes as they occur. We may find ourselves needing to move away from an area we have lived in for years, losing contact with some friends and getting closer to others, inviting new people into our lives, shifting our professional identities, handling financial challenges, and making other substantive changes.

Some changes ReBalancer can anticipate and plan for, while others are unknowable until they happen. To better deal with uncertainty, ReBalancer looks for ways to become more responsive to the needs of the moment as they arise, such as mindfulness and self-soothing activities. (See Chapters 12-13, "Embrace Change" and "Mix in Mindfulness.")

Revisiting the PCI can remind us of what kept us balanced in the past, and returning to some of those activities may help us weather this harder time. (See Chapter 15, "Stay Sane with the Personal Craziness Index.")

Tools such as the Medicine Wheel may help identify basic needs. The Miracle Question can help open a window into the new tomorrow. The Circles of Problems and Resources may be helpful in mapping out a path to recovery. (See Chapter 4, "Assess and Plan.")

To reduce the stress of change, ReBalancer may recruit helpers. A counselor or spiritual advisor can facilitate processing our feelings, a financial advisor can assist in dealing with economic situations brought on by the loss, and ReBalancer can delegate some tasks to friends and family members.

4. Restore

ReBalancer executes the plan, patching up our cuts, icing our bruises, wrapping our injured hands, and making sure we can see straight before we return to the fray.

With a sudden, major loss, Balancer needs ongoing support and nourishment in order to recover. ReBalancer knows this and leads us to resilience-building practices, to supportive communities, and to experimenting with new ways to live.

Rebalancing actions can be roughly divided into two categories: "being" and "doing." "Doing" actions are usually outward-directed—actions we carry out in the world. "Being" actions are inner-focused. They help us better understand feelings, needs, our new situation, and who we are now that things have changed.

When we've experienced a major, permanent loss, after the must-do "doing" actions have been completed, ReBalancer focuses on "being."

Radical acceptance of our new situation and what has brought us there is the beginning of restoring balance. With radical acceptance, we don't struggle against reality. We open ourselves to the pain we are feeling about the loss of our relationship or the death of someone close to us, and we allow this pain its due.

At the same time, to help us bear this pain, ReBalancer reminds us to practice self-compassion. Self-compassion is treating ourselves with the compassion and kindness we would give to a close friend who was going through the kind of suffering we are experiencing. It can feel like a direct infusion of love from one part of ourselves to the part that needs it most. (See Chapter 12, "Embrace Change.")

However, ReBalancer knows that we can't limit ourselves to receiving compassion only from ourselves.

In all Hero's Journey stories, the heroes find allies and fellow travelers along the way. Recovering from a major loss is no exception. ReBalancer knows that connecting with community provides a safety net for the essential self.

For most of us, support groups composed of people going through a similar loss are helpful parts of the recovery journey. But a spiritual or religious community, a local community center, a group of friends, or even a recreational group can provide comfort we can count on.

This comfort is not the same as the comfort of the relationship we have lost, and the community doesn't replace this intimate connection, but it does let us float on the supportive cushion of people who care about us even in the darkest times, and it reminds us that we are not alone, and that our lives will continue to evolve. (See Chapter 11, "Build Connections and Support.")

Another aspect of the restoration process following a major loss involves awakening parts of ourselves that have been dormant.

We may discover a desire to deepen a spiritual practice, start or restart a creative activity, or both. To restore balance, ReBalancer assists us in building a new life that intertwines what we bring forward from our previous life with what we discover. ReBalancer reminds us of interests from the past that we may have set aside and encourages us to try them again, and also to venture into areas previously unexplored. Mindfulness practices help us get to know who we are becoming, in the present moment. Combining mindfulness, community, and creativity yields a whole greater than the sum of its parts. (See Chapter 12, "Embrace Change.")

An example: Following a major breakup and a brief period of unsuccessful dating, I realized I was not yet prepared for a new relationship, nor did I know how to find one. After a few false starts, I gradually came to understand and to accept that this was a time to go inward instead, and to deepen my spiritual practice, my literary and artistic sides, and connections to friends and family. By the time I was ready for a new relationship, I was not the person I had been before, and the relationship I found was a better match for the person I had become.

After a major loss, we may also need to experiment. We are not quite the same person we were before, and our changed selves may need, want, and desire activities, people, and situations that are different from the ones we had before. New interests may arise, and from them we may forge new friendships with people who are more akin to who we are now. (See Chapter 6, "The Experiment.")

5. Integrate

ReBalancer teaches Balancer what it's gleaned from the struggle, better preparing us for UnBalancer's mean left hook and fancy footwork.

The return to balance after a period of chronic stress can sometimes feel like a fresh start, accompanied by radical changes in lifestyle, but more often we return to an improved version of the life we lived before.

After a major loss, however, the return is almost always transformative.

We may find new relationships that are very different from the ones we lost. We may reconnect with spiritual and creative practices we left behind long ago, or that we freshly discover. We may make substantial changes to career, location, and roles within our social circles. Even our appearance may change, more accurately reflecting our new direction.

This recovery-as-rebirth is called **post-traumatic growth**. Post-traumatic growth is positive change that comes from struggling through a traumatic event or major life crisis.

People who experience post-traumatic growth can develop an increased sense of purpose, a broader appreciation for life, closer relationships, greater empathy, a deeper sense of spiritual connection, and a sense that if they can survive what happened to them, they can survive anything. The extent of growth is often proportional to the degree of crisis.

On the other side of recovery from a major loss, ReBalancer guides us into integrating the parts of ourselves that have been awakened in the grieving process with the person we had been before.

Some examples of post-traumatic growth:

- Following a near-death experience, I dropped out of the English PhD program I was in at the time and returned to graduate school to become a therapist.

- Following the death of her husband, an attorney friend attended a bereavement group with a focus on writing, and evolved into a new identity centering on creative writing.

- Following his difficult divorce, another friend quit his job as an administrator and started a foundation to help handicapped children.

6. Monitor/Maintain

Moving forward, Balancer keeps a closer watch on UnBalancer, and also maintains new-and-improved strategies to better equip us to emerge the victor in our next encounter with UnBalancer.

Once we have recovered our equanimity and settled into our integrated lives, it's important to continue the practices and activities that helped us get there. We are no longer our older, more familiar selves and our old styles of interacting with others and of relating to ourselves won't quite fit anymore.

ReBalancer passes on to Balancer everything we have learned on this journey and Balancer makes sure that we retain what we have gained on our healing path. We re-do the PCI, making note of what now gives us stability and fulfillment, so that our new selves can be more resilient in the event of future difficult events.

We have become whole again, but in a different way than we were before the loss.

Addendum:
When UnBalancer is the Hero

In the midst of chaos, there is also opportunity.
- **Sun Tzu**, *The Art of War*

Throughout this book, UnBalancer has been characterized as an enemy, and often that's how it seems.

But UnBalancer is also a necessary part of the yin/yang of our lives.

Much of the time, we need to stay within the parameters of our created lives. Balancer and ReBalancer are good at helping us do that. But sometimes we need to end one thing so we can begin another. And that's where UnBalancer's tendency to destroy comes in.

What William Blake, the radical romantic poet of the Renaissance, called the Creator and the Destroyer are both as essential to our personal evolution as they have been to evolution itself.

Without its opposite, the Destroyer, the Creator would stagnate.

Most of the world's religions and mythologies have a force that destroys the old to make room for the new. Hinduism has Shiva the Destroyer. The Old Testament God flooded the world so humanity could start fresh. The Titans of the Greeks had to be overthrown so the Gods could take over.

This creating/destroying/creating cycle has also been the pattern of evolution on our planet. We and multitudes of other mammals may never have come into being had an asteroid not made life impossible for dinosaurs.

In our individual lives, it's also sometimes necessary for one door to close so another can open.

We all need to leave home to start our adult lives. Some marriages have to end so more fulfilling ones can begin. Jobs sometimes must end to make room for new, better ones to arise. Major medical events and other traumas at first seem to take something from us, but the post-traumatic growth that often follows can sometimes give us far more.

When the path we've been on comes to an abrupt end, we can stop and look around and ask what we can do *now*.

Understanding the opportunities implicit in loss came to me most clearly following a near-death experience. That afternoon, lying in a hospital bed with what I thought was a minor illness, I was cranky and irritable, annoyed with the nurses and my girlfriend because of the inconvenience of being away from everything that seemed vitally important to achieving success as a college professor and novelist. A couple of hours later, I was fighting not to succeed in that career, but to stay alive.

From that moment forward, I was on a different path. Would my life have been more valuable if UnBalancer hadn't intervened and I'd written that novel and completed that PhD? Or has the range of experiences since then been enriching in ways that could not have occurred had I remained on my original path? It's hard to know for sure, but I can say that the years since then have been the most emotionally enriching period of my life.

Since my own radical unbalancing, I have seen dozens of examples among my friends, family, and clients of UnBalancer slamming one door shut, only to have another, better door open.

As Arlo Guthrie put it, "You can't have a light without a dark to stick it in."

The ultimate balance is the one between UnBalancer and Balancer. When we radically accept that the path we're on is, indeed, ours, it becomes a yellow brick road, leading us to our personal Oz.

You must be swift as the wind, dense as the forest, rapacious as fire, steadfast like a mountain, mysterious as night and mighty as thunder.

- **Sun Tzu**, *The Art of War*

Acknowledgments

This book would not have been possible without the help and support of many people. These are some to whom I'd particularly like to give thanks.

Barrie Levine for her support throughout this project, and for her keen editing eye.

Stephanie Bond, whose illustration talents and diligence brought the Cast of Characters to life.

Dominque Chappard, for releasing her "Al the Stickman" drawings into the public domain. They inspired many of the illustrations in this book.

My clients, from whom I have learned more about balance than I can adequately express.

My early reviewers, who helped me see what was truly helpful and what I needed to revise.

The readers who responded to bits and pieces of this book when they first appeared on my blog, phototransformations.com.

My teachers, including Jack Clarke, Linda Keuhl, Herbert Mason, Jim Grant, Leroy Kelly, Stephen Merther, Thich Nhat Hanh, Glenn Saxe, Dusty Miller, Joan Klagsbrun, John Bell, and the many others whose names I may have neglected to mention.

Insoo Kim Berg and Steven de Shazer, for creating and developing the Miracle Question.

Rick Hanson, for his ideas on rewiring the brain as described in his book *Buddha's Brain: The Practical Neuroscience of Happiness, Love, and Wisdom* and his website rickhanson.net.

Tara Brach, for her Radical Acceptance practices, as described in her book *Radical Acceptance: Embracing Your Life With the Heart of a Buddha* and her website tarabrach.com.

Kristin Neff, for her self-compassion practices, as described in her book *Self-Compassion: The Proven Power of Being Kind to Yourself* and her website self-compassion.org.

Jack Kornfield, for his Forgiveness Meditation, as displayed on his website jackkornfield.com.

Patrick J. Carnes, for his Personal Craziness Index concept, as described in his book *A Gentle Path through the Twelve Steps: The Classic Guide for All People in the Process of Recovery.*

Steven Pressfield, for his characterization of Resistance—a confederate of UnBalancer—in his book *The War of Art.*

THANK YOU!

We have come to the end of our journey. I hope you have benefited from our time together, and that the lessons learned will continue to help you stay ahead of UnBalancer.

Before you go, I'd like to ask for your help in spreading the word and furthering the cause.

These days, UnBalancer seems to have built up a head of steam, but that doesn't mean it can't be derailed. I wrote *The Art of Balance* to add one more arrow to the quivers of my fellow warriors in the Battle for Balance.

If you like what you've found here, please tell your friends and family. And, to get the word out more generally, it would be terrific if you'd write a review on Amazon.com.

- To leave a review on Amazon, go to:
  amazon.com/dp/product-reviews/B078SY89K4

- To leave a review on Goodreads, go to:
  goodreads.com/book/show/37677566

- To get *The Art of Balance* cheat sheet, go to:
  transformationspress.org/resources/nonfiction-resources

- To join the Facebook group "The Balance Lab,"
  go to: **facebook.com/groups/balancelab**

- To see new tips, works in progress, and receive other bonuses, go to: **phototransformations.com**

- To learn about my book *Paths to Wholeness: Fifty-Two Flower Mandalas*, go to: **amazon.com/dp/0984699406**

- To learn about other books by Transformations Press, go to: **transformationspress.org**

ABOUT THE AUTHOR

David J. Bookbinder is a psychotherapist, life coach, and photographer.

He came to psychotherapy after a transformative near-death experience shifted him toward art and healing. As a coach and therapist, for the past 15 years he has helped people find balance, build resilience, overcome fear, and expand their lives.

David has been taking photographs since he was six. His award-winning Flower Mandala images were inspired by the paintings of Georgia O'Keeffe and the flower photographs of Harold Feinstein, with whom he briefly studied.

In addition to *The Art of Balance: Staying Sane in an Insane World* and *Paths to Wholeness: Fifty-Two Flower Mandalas*, he is the author of two coloring books for adults based on his Flower Mandalas, a book about American folk music, and three books about computer software.

David lives and works north of Boston and is a native of Buffalo, New York.